Planning and Using Skills Inventory Systems

Planning and Using Skills Inventory Systems

Richard A. Kaumeyer, Jr.

VAN NOSTRAND REINHOLD COMPANY
NEW YORK   CINCINNATI   ATLANTA   DALLAS   SAN FRANCISCO
LONDON   TORONTO   MELBOURNE

Van Nostrand Reinhold Company Regional Offices:
New York   Cincinnati   Atlanta   Dallas   San Francisco

Van Nostrand Reinhold Company International Offices:
London   Toronto   Melbourne

Copyright © 1979 by Litton Educational Publishing, Inc.

Library of Congress Catalog Card Number: 78-25959
ISBN: 0-442-24240-9

All rights reserved. No part of this work covered by the copyright hereon may be reproduced or used in any form or by any means—graphic, electronic, or mechanical, including photocopying, recording, taping, or information storage and retrieval systems—without permission of the publisher.

Manufactured in the United States of America

Published by Van Nostrand Reinhold Company
135 West 50th Street, New York, N. Y. 10020

Published simultaneously in Canada by Van Nostrand Reinhold Ltd.

15 14 13 12 11 10 9 8 7 6 5 4 3 2 1

Library of Congress Cataloging in Publication Data

Kaumeyer, Jr., Richard A
  Planning and using skills inventory systems.

  1. Manpower planning—Data processing. 2. Skilled labor—Inventories. I. Title.
  HF5549.5.M3K38   658.31′28′02854   78-25959
  ISBN 0-442-24240-9

To Carol

PREFACE

Skills inventory systems have been in use for many years. Recently, changes in technology and computer systems have made their use more feasible. As smaller firms have had access to new processing techniques, both manual and machine, the interest in skills inventory systems has increased.

Most organizations either have an inventory system or have seriously considered the use of one. The topic is continuously on the agendas of professional and technical clubs and organizations representing the areas of management, personnel, human resources, planning, etc. Those who have operated, or been involved with inventories are in heavy demand for guest-speaking engagements. Vendors and consultants have recognized the skills inventory area as a growing market with present and future possibilities.

All organizations are changing at an ever-increasing rate. New jobs are being created, and old ones deleted, on a regular basis. No area is immune to this change, be it government agencies, educational institutions or private business. All are changing and evolving in shorter time frames. Twenty-five years ago a person could choose a career field and assume he/she would retire in that area. Today, many positions have changed so dramatically that we cannot recognize the same job after five years. Projecting this forward, most knowledgeable people realize that their career path must be flexible to grow and progress.

This change not only has impact on people, but on the organizations which they form. An individual can no longer be put into a slot with his/her path of progression plotted over his/her working life. As new positions are added and deleted, organizations must be able to fill these. New combinations and groupings of skills are required. To survive in this environment an organization has to be able to quickly identify its changing needs, and match these with the skills of its people. Those organizations which do this most successfully are going to accomplish their missions and grow and prosper.

A skills inventory is one method of matching the skills of people to existing requirements. It allows for flexibility as the mix changes. It provides a tool for examining the various possible combinations and alternatives that are occurring. The career path of the future is not a constant, and has not been for many years. Those people and organizations holding this premise are deluding themselves.

This book is designed for those who are interested in setting up a skills inventory system, and the order of the chapters is intended to serve as a guide to doing so. An effort has been made to guide those making the initial decision through an orderly thought process. The pros and cons of various types of systems and alternatives have been explored.

The book is also designed to assist those who may already have a skills inventory system, but are thinking of modifying or improving it. Systems must evolve and grow along with the people and organizations they serve. Every organization which has an inventory system must be alert to changes and opportunities which occur, so that they may continue to improve what they have. There are many concepts and alternatives to systems design and use which are explored here. It is hoped that this book will provide some new ideas and guidance to those involved in modifying their existing systems.

A good deal of time is devoted to dealing with outside vendor consultants and the related contracting process. Today the "make or buy" decision is one of the major ones faced by management. Purchasing either an entire system or enlisting outside aid in designing one is becoming an accepted practice.

There are a number of reasons why we are now turning to outside firms and organizations for aid in the systems area. One reason stems from the nature of technology, which in itself experiences rapid change and evolution. No one organization can hope to stay current with all the advances and changes, and vendor/consultants provide this link. They can become specialists in their segments of the market, and be alert to those items of significance.

Another reason management is going to outside areas for assistance is the staff commitment to internal development. Either the skilled people are already available, or we have to hire them. Most organizations do not possess total expertise in the areas of skills inventories. This means either hiring such skills or going to a vendor/consultant. The hire decision is becoming more of a commitment than it was in the past. Whereas at one time when a specialist's talents were no longer required, the organization could immediately dismiss him or her, today society no longer condones the layoff procedure to the degree it once did. This book is aimed at the person who is interested in skills inventories, but who is not necessarily a computer expert. Care has been taken to avoid technical systems jargon. Wherever possible these terms have been converted to everyday English. Although this may make the reading a bit dull for the expert, we hope it will make it of more value to non-technical managers. These are the people who most frequently are involved at all levels of the decision-making process. It is hoped that this down-to-earth approach will provide a clearer picture, and will be an aid in their decision-making endeavors.

The material presented here is a compilation of many years of experience dealing with various aspects of inventories. Every effort was made to avoid any personal bias. It is hoped this has been achieved. The end product is aimed at shedding light, in layman's language, on the planning and use of skills inventory systems.

Richard A. Kaumeyer, Jr.
Canoga Park, California

CONTENTS

Preface		vii
1	SKILLS INVENTORY SYSTEMS AND DEVELOPMENT	1
2	PARTS OF A CLASSICAL SYSTEM	19
3	KEY WORDS–THE HEART OF THE SYSTEM	30
4	INVENTORY INPUT FORMS	43
5	INVENTORY STORAGE AND PROCESSING	56
6	INVENTORY OUTPUT FORMS	65
7	INTERNAL DESIGN CONSIDERATIONS	83
8	EXTERNAL PURCHASE CONSIDERATIONS	101
9	COMBINING INTERNAL DESIGN WITH EXTERNAL PURCHASE	117
10	THE IMPACT OF TECHNOLOGY	130
11	COST CONSIDERATIONS	145
12	MAXIMUM USE OF THE SYSTEM	168
13	WHY INVENTORIES HAVE FAILED	181
14	MANPOWER PLANNING AND THE FUTURE	191
15	SUMMARY AND CONCLUSION	207
Index		217

Planning and Using Skills Inventory Systems

1
SKILLS INVENTORY SYSTEMS AND DEVELOPMENT

DEFINITION OF SKILLS INVENTORY SYSTEMS

The first question which should be raised is what is a skills inventory system? In its most basic sense it is a system that allows matching of an individual's experience, education and preference with a task or function to be performed. We might better understand what a skills inventory is by seeing one of its products. A sample employee data sheet or biography is shown in Figure 1.1.

Skills inventories are not necessarily specific selection tools. Skills inventories are personnel search tools that many times use computers to aid in improving response time. They are used by reducing a large population to one of manageable size.

For instance, if we had a firm of two thousand employees and needed someone who had three years of tax experience, a CPA and spoke Spanish, a skills inventory could be of assistance. The objective of the inventory would be to produce a list of those employees who had the specified experience, professional certificate and language capability (Figure 1.2).

The activity here involves the reduction of the population of two thousand to a manageable number of say ten or twelve employees. It would be at this stage that the actual selection decision would be made as to the individual person to whom the specific job or assignment would be given. The actual selection decision is made from the list provided by the skills inventory, but the skills inventory does not make the selection.

SKILLS INVENTORY

Employee Name: I. M. Nameless
Employee Number: 28036

Date Printed: 1-1-78
Department: 319

KEY WORDS

Word	Description	Activity
1. Accounting	Tax accounting	Supervising and analyzing
2. Bookkeeping	General ledger	Supervising
3. Auditing	Computer records	Analyzing

WORK EXPERIENCE

	Description	From	To
1.	Chief Tax Accountant at XYZ Stores	1973	1978
2.	Bookkeeper at XYZ Manufacturing	1965	1973
3.	Auditing Trainee at XY Bank	1964	1965

EDUCATION

Degree	Major	Year
1. MBA	Business Administration	1964
2. BS	Accounting	1962

SPECIAL COURSES

	Course	Date
1.	Management theory	1974
2.	Business planning	1971
3.	Computer audits	1965

MEMBERSHIPS

1. American Accounting Society
2. American Management Association

LANGUAGES

Name	Fluency
1. Spanish	Fluent
2. French	Read

POSITION PREFERENCE

1. Accounting
2. Auditing

LOCATION PREFERENCE

1. San Francisco
2. San Diego

HOBBIES

1. Bridge
2. Amateur radio
3. Boating

LICENSES

Name	Date
1. CPA	1965

Employee Signature: _____ Personnel Department: _____
Date: _____ Date: _____

Figure 1-1

SKILLS INVENTORY SEARCH LISTING

Employee Identification Number	Employee Name	Experience	Professional Certification	Language	Language Proficiency
12345	R. J. Gonzales	Tax	CPA	Spanish	Fluent
50343	A. R. Friend	Tax	CPA	Spanish	Fluent
23451	R. L. Smith	Tax	CPA	Spanish	Fluent
32415	R. J. Thomas	Tax	CPA	Spanish	Fluent
25451	S. J. Brown	Tax	CPA	Spanish	Fluent
50000	R. S. Green	Tax	CPA	Spanish	Fluent
43001	B. J. Frank	Tax	CPA	Spanish	Fluent
32221	C. J. Gomez	Tax	CPA	Spanish	Fluent
28762	E. C. Roberts	Tax	CPA	Spanish	Fluent

Note: The list identifies all the employees with the specific skills being sought. In addition, if even more detail on these people were required we might also attach the individual employee data sheets or biographies shown in Figure 1.1.

Figure 1-2

4 Planning and Using Skills Inventory Systems

Skills inventories also can be a valuable tool in training and development. Here we are trying to find both skills that exist and also skills that are lacking in a group of employees so that we may provide the the latter with the necessary training. If an organization is going to computerize a section of its operation, or add a computerized function to its existing operation, knowing who has experience can be of significant value. These people can be identified as potential trainers as the new functions are introduced. In the event that no one has had any prior experience, finding this out is just as important. Here we may wish to institute an entire training program, since no prior knowledge exists. A pictorial description of this process is shown in Figure 1.3.

Another important function of an inventory can be to identify preferences of employees both as to future job and work location. Often the company and the employee can both be working very hard in this area with totally conflicting goals. The company may be striving hard to groom the employee for additional responsibility in the accounting department while the employee is studying nights to prepare to move into the marketing area. This may seem to be a waste, which it is, and properly identifying preferences can aid in avoiding this conflict.

This same situation occurs not just with job preferences, but also with location preference. One employee is being moved to meet a very real company operating requirement. This person is not interested in the transfer and goes along with it purely to keep a paycheck coming in. Often, as a result of the transfer the person will have started efforts to find other employment. The end result is a valuable employee lost or so dissatisfied that performance is markedly affected. It is not uncommon that another employee not only wants the move, but would view it positively as a means of achieving one of his/her work related goals.

Skills inventories also have value for research purposes. The greater the participation in the inventory, of course, the better the statistical results from any surveys conducted. Most inventories with voluntary participation of employees never have one hundred percent participation. However, if the amount of employee participation

INVENTORIES AND TRAINING

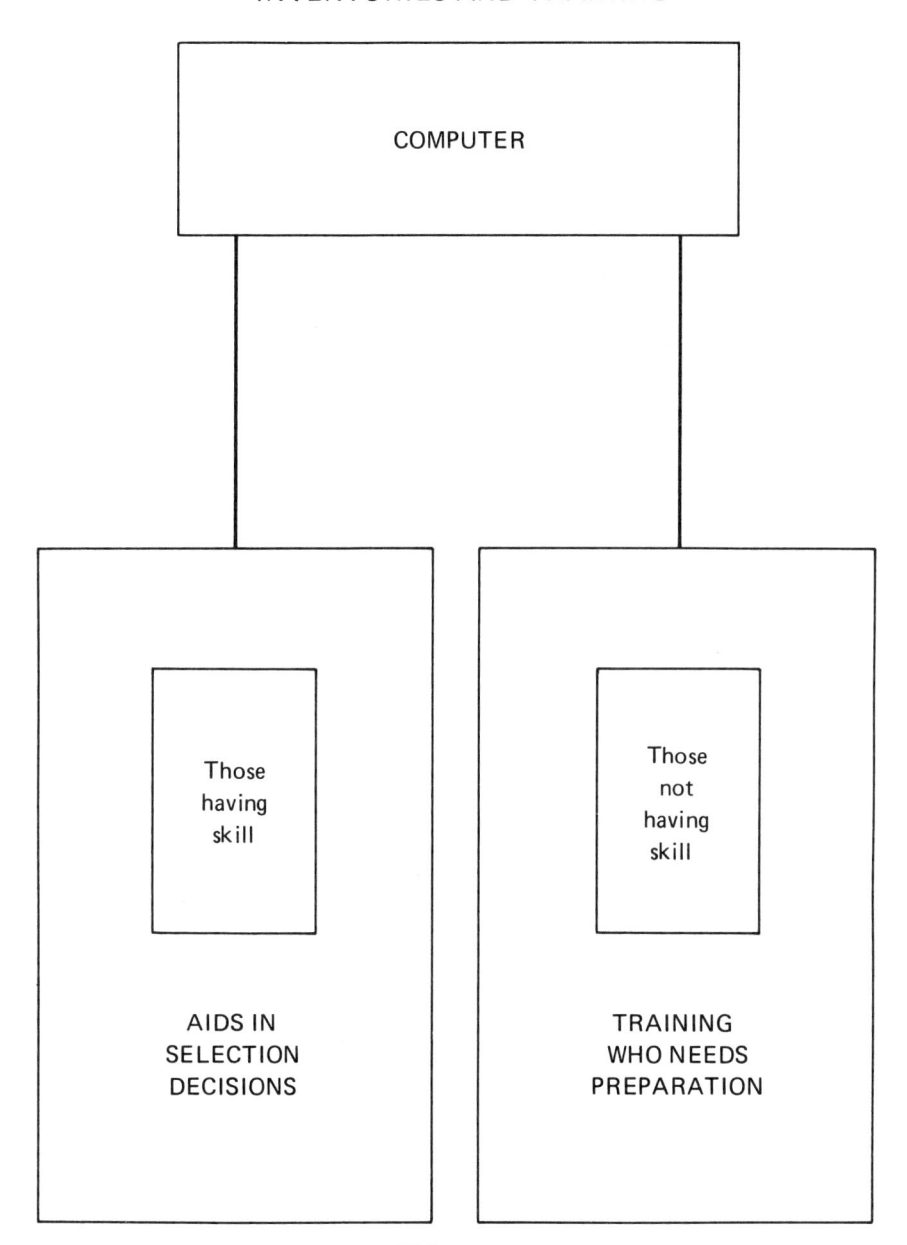

```
┌─────────────────────────────┐
│          COMPUTER           │
└─────────────────────────────┘
         │            │
┌────────┴──────┐ ┌───┴──────────┐
│  ┌─────────┐  │ │  ┌─────────┐ │
│  │  Those  │  │ │  │  Those  │ │
│  │ having  │  │ │  │   not   │ │
│  │  skill  │  │ │  │ having  │ │
│  │         │  │ │  │  skill  │ │
│  └─────────┘  │ │  └─────────┘ │
│    AIDS IN    │ │   TRAINING   │
│   SELECTION   │ │  WHO NEEDS   │
│   DECISIONS   │ │ PREPARATION  │
└───────────────┘ └──────────────┘
```

Figure 1-3

is known, accurate surveys can still be conducted. Survey information can be of particular value for many purposes including internal studies, exchanging information with other companies, government contracts, etc. In fact, information regarding internal skills and education is mandatory in bidding on many large government contracts.

Recently, these inventory systems have been required as part of Affirmative Action plans and agreements, by government agencies such as the Treasury Department, Equal Employment Opportunity Commission, etc., that are involved in Affirmative Action compliance and enforcement. The effort here is to insure that all possible candidates are reviewed for possible selection for any opportunities for advancement or training. The requirements in the affirmative action area have added increased stimulus to the interest in, and use of skills inventory systems. In effect, every government contractor is required to give very serious consideration to possibly utilizing these methods.

USE AND DEVELOPMENT

What has been the development and use of skills inventories in business in the past? It would be safe to say that the concept of skills inventories is usually considered very early in a firm's development. As soon as a firm or organization reaches a size where individual capabilities are not readily known, the search is on to match jobs with people. An estimated relationship between the size of a firm and the use of inventories is shown in Figure 1.4.

In many firms the personnel department or even a manpower group (now referred to as a staff planning or human resource planning group) has been assigned the task of matching people and jobs. In certain instances people working in these areas have become quite valuable strictly through their knowledge of the organization and the people in it. They perform their wizardry of matchmaking by knowing who can do what, and physically where the people are located in the company. However, as firms grow (or these knowl-

USE OF SKILLS INVENTORIES

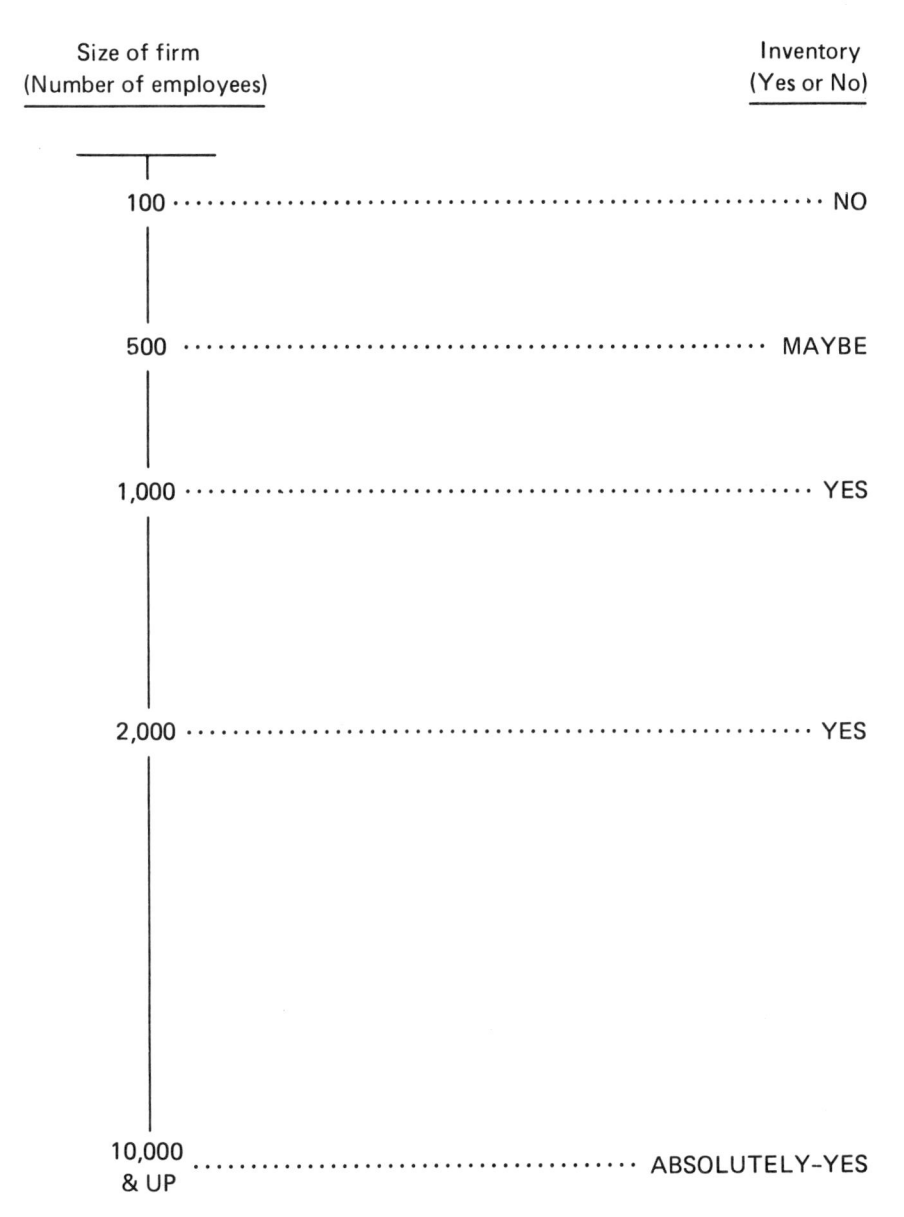

Size of firm (Number of employees)	Inventory (Yes or No)
100	NO
500	MAYBE
1,000	YES
2,000	YES
10,000 & UP	ABSOLUTELY-YES

Figure 1-4

edgeable people leave or retire) we turn to other more technically reliable sources to do the matchmaking.

Business certainly has not been the originator, nor the forerunner, in facing either the problem of locating internal talent or in developing concepts of skills inventories to solve the problem. Over many years governments and related military organizations have been using, experimenting, and dealing with inventories and having varying degrees of success.

In comparison to government, business has lagged in the area of skills inventories. The first reason is that governments have achieved size and diversity earlier than most business organizations. Large armies, warships, etc. have been staffed with varying skill levels over long spans of time. Civil bureaucracy has expanded, but not with the measurable level of skills seen in military organizations. In the military most tasks are defined down to the finest detail. In fact, many times these details or steps are listed by number; hence, the term doing something "by the numbers."

Secondly, in addition to the needs which come from pure growth in size, two additional occurrences have made it necessary for skills inventories to be used by business. One reason is the frequent dealing by business with the government and military. This reached a critical point in the United States during and after World War II. To ensure quality work on contracts, business was asked to supply information in ever increasing detail on the quality and capabilities of its staff. Many contract specifications required lists of the education and experience levels of the groups working on various types of technical proposals.

At the same time the cost of labor was continuing to rise and technical advances were causing greater specialization of the labor force. These narrow fields of specialization were brought home during the late 1950s and through the 1960s. This was the age of the cold war and the space race, with the moon and planets as the targets and the sky no longer the limit.

During this period, fields of work became compartmentalized. Previously an engineer was an engineer, but now they were further separated into fields such as mechanical, electrical, chemical etc. Also, at this point in time the structure was even further reduced to multiple types of specialities within these broad fields (e.g. hydromechanical). The specialties became so important that the other broader terms were abandoned when preparing bids for contracts.

In the past, just having, let us say an engineering degree, qualified a person to do engineering work. This moved to an era where having a degree in a specific field of engineering qualified one to at least do work in that field of engineering. This further dissolved into having to have a specialty in that particular field to perform that task. In essence, being able to use degrees as a determining factor in one's ability to perform was for all intents and purposes lost. The degree might be one limiting factor, but it had become so broad that other factors had to be included to provide any meaningful criteria.

THE ENTRANCE OF COMPUTER TECHNOLOGY

This same time period was spawning another item which was to lend itself to skills inventories coming onto the scene. This same technology that was making the skills more detailed and creating multiple areas of specialization was also advancing the computer technology. Computers were not only being used more, but their use and access was being extended to users of all sizes, and even to those with limited financial resources. No longer were the government, military or giant conglomerates the only ones able to use computers.

This was also the time when the computer was freed from being strictly the tool of the scientist or the mathematician. With the reduced cost, and ability to handle large volumes of data, its use soon appeared in other areas of business. It was readily employed in financial reporting and the handling of both intricate and routine payroll processing. It was not long before it wandered into the personnel departments. Why not? If large volumes of mathematical calculations could be handled, and dollars and payrolls accounted for, why not track and account for the human resources?

THE EVOLUTION OF COMPUTERS

The evolution in personnel goes through the basic number counting of knowing how many in what department, to present day considerations for career pathing. It was, however, at an early stage that computers were considered for application to the problems of skills inventories.

Computers and skills inventories could be considered an ideal match. People have multiple and varied backgrounds with many combinations of experience, education and preferences. Each individual has a large number combination. Couple this with several thousand or even several hundred thousand people and you have a task which is impossible to deal with by hand.

It was the government and military that were, again, first able to utilize the computer in the personnel field and in skills inventories. As computers became more available to business through greater efficiency, reduction in cost and proven cost effective value, they were applied to the related personnel and inventory uses.

Computer technology has continued to evolve and advance. With these changes have come enhancements which have made applications in the personnel field both feasible and cost effective. One of the most important factors to the personnel manager has been the advance in turnaround time which has increased along with the computer technology advances. This factor has been of significant importance since personnel departments service line organizations. The line will use the services of personnel or any other staff organization only if they are responsive and timely.

Sorting of punched cards was slow and laborious. Batch processing under old methods was faster, but still did not provide the rapid response desired. Even this became slowed further as the system became overloaded with higher priority requests. A major innovation in computers which has helped the response time for skills inventories has been the use of computer terminals in a real-time mode or environment.

This has allowed the personnel specialist to receive a search request and go directly to a typewriter terminal and enquire directly and immediately into the computer. The search criteria can be fed in, and the listing of people printed out, without going through elaborate request procedures or through extended waiting periods.

This has had a very positive effect on skills inventories and their use by management. Answers can be had at once and not several weeks or days after the initial questions which created the search requirement. This availability and accessibility encourages the use of any search system and has provided a vital enhancement to skills inventory files.

The alternative to computer terminal files is to have printed external listings in alphabetical order. These will allow ready access to information outside a computer system. The problem here is that these listings can become cumbersome if the file is large, and cross-matching has to be pre-determined. (See the development in the use of computers for skills inventories shown in Figure 1.5.) In other words, possible search criteria have to be defined sufficiently ahead of time to put them in some logical list. It is never completely feasible to identify all the possible sequences ahead of time. This fact in itself creates built-in systems limitations.

The past can sometimes be a good base from which to project or forecast future occurrences. The area of skills inventories is no exception. We have just gone over the past and present development and uses of the inventory concepts.

To a large extent the use will be tied to the continued development of computer technology. Theoretically, as more efficient design reduces the cost of using computers, the use of inventories will increase. At the present time large files can be stored and detailed searches performed. One of the major limiting factors is the cost of doing this.

Technology will continue to advance. Theoretically, storage of information on computer systems can be expanded almost to infinity. New and as yet unthought of search techniques will be developed that will allow the costs to be reduced from dollars to a fraction of a dollar (See Figure 1.6).

These concepts may seem farfetched, but if you look at developments in the last decade, these possibilities are certainly within the realm of reasonable consideration. Look, for instance, at what has happened to the calculator over the past few years. It used to be that to perform any amount of complicated activity such as multiplication or division a person had to go to a large and cumbersome piece of equipment.

Many may remember the weight of this equipment which ranged

SKILLS INVENTORY DEVELOPMENT

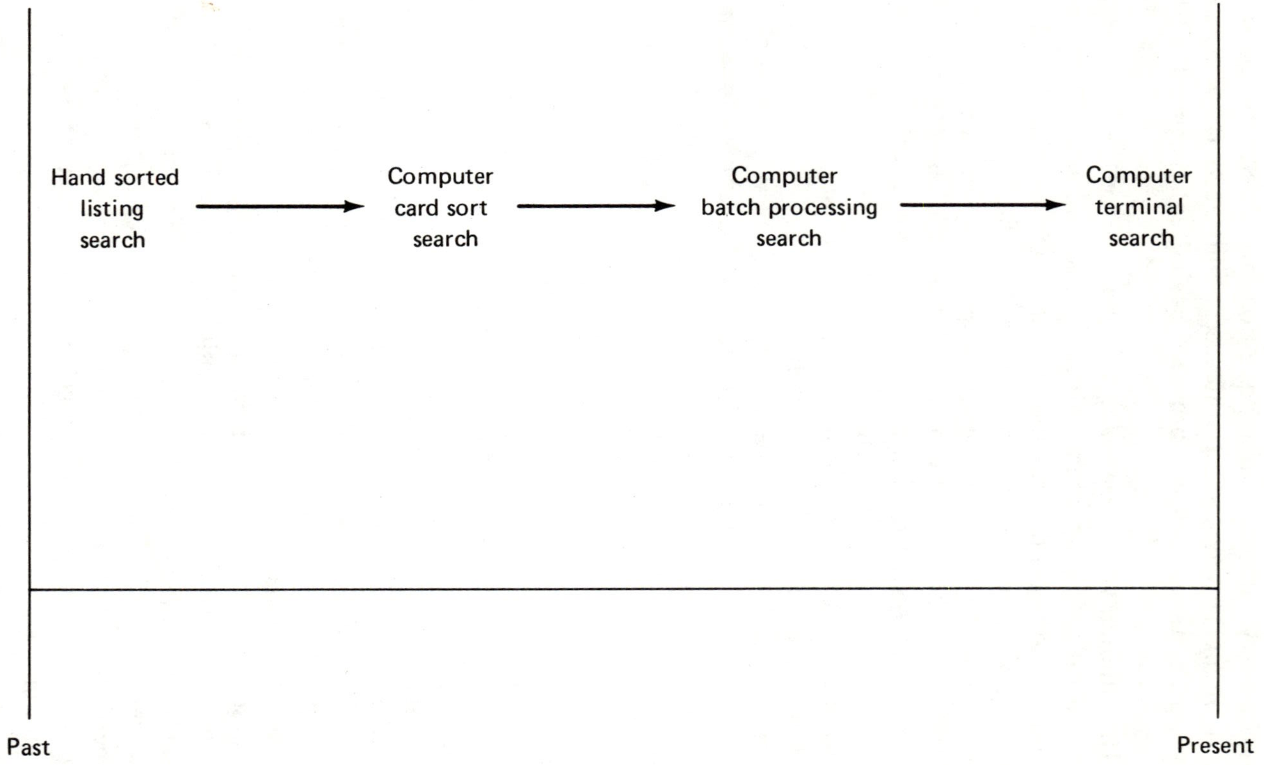

Past → Hand sorted listing search → Computer card sort search → Computer batch processing search → Computer terminal search → Present

Figure 1-5

Skills Inventory Systems and Development

COSTS TO USE
SKILLS INVENTORIES

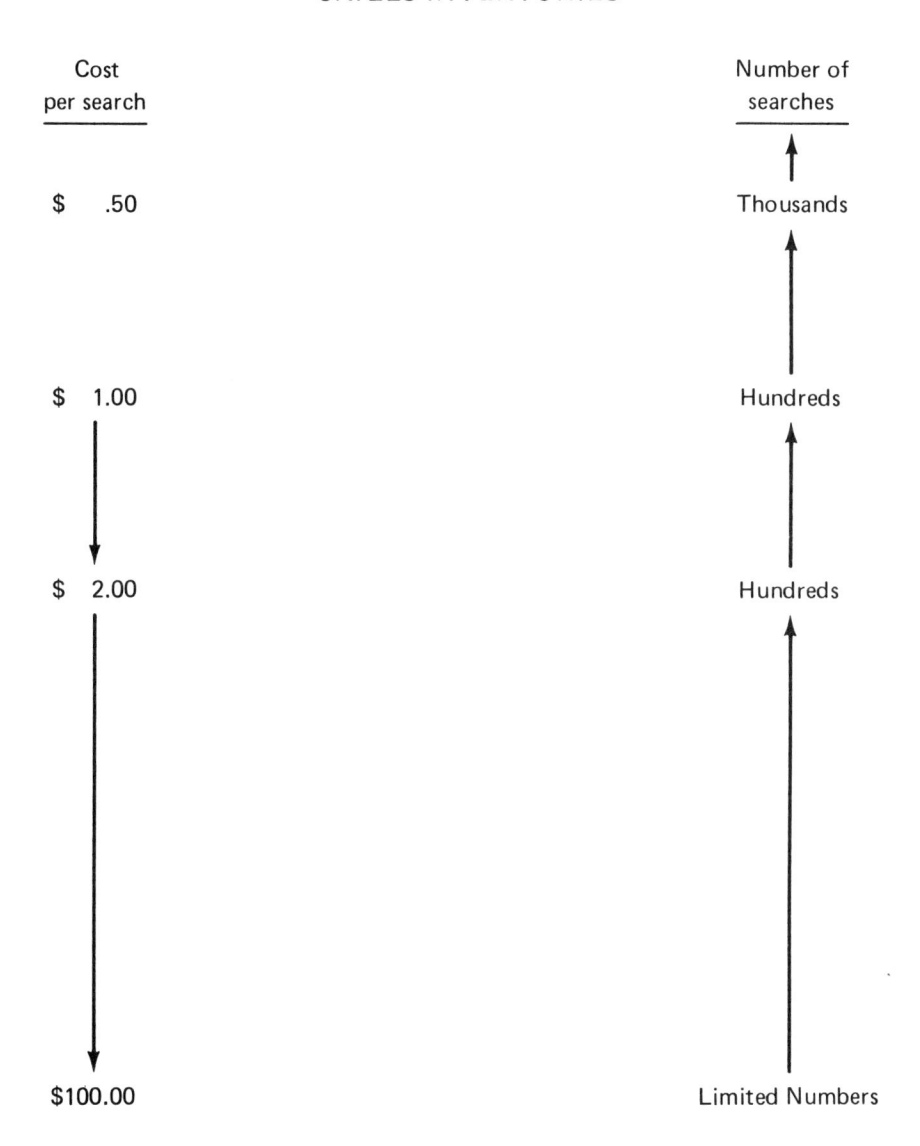

Cost per search		Number of searches
$ .50		Thousands
$ 1.00		Hundreds
$ 2.00		Hundreds
$100.00		Limited Numbers

As costs are reduced to cents per search, the use is increased dramatically.

Figure 1-6

to forty plus pounds. The machines were mounted on trays with wheels so they could be moved from one area of the office to another, and the noise level produced in operating one of these would be considered "noise pollution" today. The cost was that of a major outlay for office equipment.

In this case, the future being today, we have taken advantage of technological advances in the area of calculators. In size they have been miniaturized. Some are the size of wristwatches and can be activated by a pen type stylus. Most are the size of a wallet and can be carried in a suit or shirt pocket. They can add, subtract, multiply, divide, in a fraction of the time previously required. In fact, they have become so advanced technically that their functions have replaced slide rules.

Their operation involves almost no noise. The cost is such that most business people own one or more of their own, as well as having access to them at the office. Even students in elementary math classes can afford them. The question now is whether in the future our youth will be able to perform simple arithmetical calculations unaided.

Miniaturization is already taking place with computers, and this has direct application to possible growth and expansion of inventory systems. If you do not believe this go into a computer room designed ten years ago, but now using current hardware. You get the feeling of a single plate on a banquet table, or a pea in a rain barrel. The room seems to dwarf the equipment (See Figure 1.7).

Computer rooms were specially built to handle the necessary under-floor electric cables, cooling pipes, etc. The rooms were to handle the then current equipment and to provide for expansion. The "expansion" has definitely occurred, since we are making ever increasing use of computers. Technology just altered the way the expansion took place. It did not take place in physical size. In fact, computers have continued to grow smaller each year. Portable computers, not terminals, that weigh under fifty pounds are now on the market. These too will grow smaller.

The cost factor is also on the down side. At one point only government or large corporations could justify the presence of

Skills Inventory Systems and Development 15

COMPUTER ROOM AND CURRENT EQUIPMENT

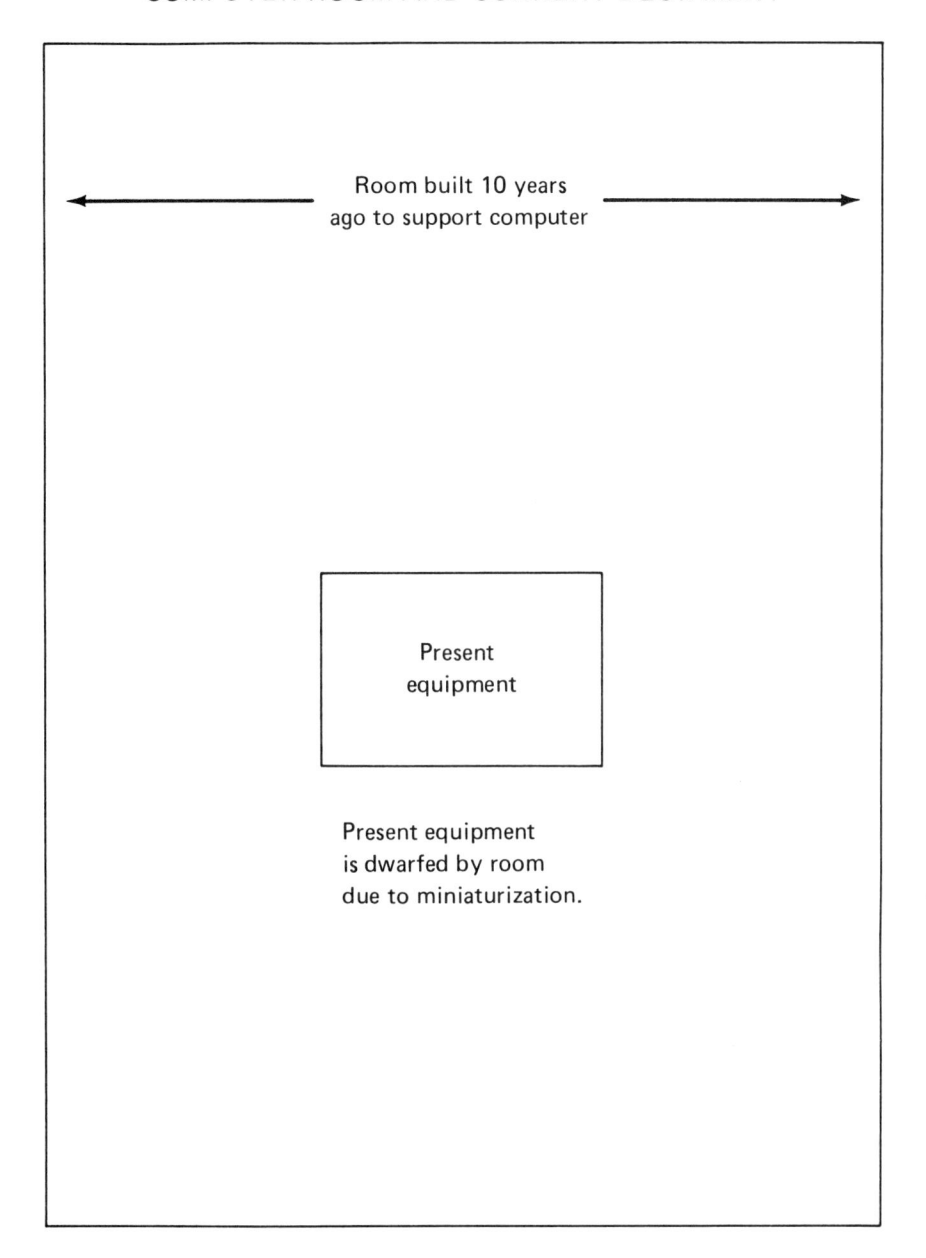

←──────── Room built 10 years ────────→
ago to support computer

Present
equipment

Present equipment
is dwarfed by room
due to miniaturization.

Figure 1-7

computers in terms of cost. Now most small firms have them and many individuals are rapidly following. There are even kits on the market, similar in nature to those used for building a stereo set from a kit, that allow a person to assemble his/her own computer. Private ownership is no longer a dream, but a reality. With this expanded use of computers can only come faster and ever increasing knowledge of computers and expanded use of them.

Twenty years ago only a limited number of colleges and universities had access to computers for research purposes. Today, it would be hard to find a college of any size that does not have multiple computer capability, both for its own business processing as well as for scientific or research and development purposes. Most business schools and scientific/engineering schools offer majors and minors in computer science and technology.

POTENTIAL BENEFITS AND PROBLEMS

The ability to have skills inventories available in most firms of any size allows better utilization of internal skills. The talents of those connected with large organizations are more easily identified to the benefit of both the organization and the employee. Overall efficiency is increased and general employee morale can be improved.

Those implementing skills inventories within companies have encountered problems outside of just the technical and operational phases which are being discussed here. These include the resistance to change and the very real concern about the centralization of data on employees. Many people fear the use of computer technology and its potential for misuse.

Firms that have successfully overcome this problem have done so by several methods. First, by being open and honest about how they intend to use the data they are collecting. Second, by publicizing those people who have benefited from participation in the system. Third, and possibly the most important of all, by making the system voluntary to the employees. In the long run this has the most positive benefit. Management style overall is tending toward employee par-

Skills Inventory Systems and Development 17

MATCHING JOBS WITH PEOPLE

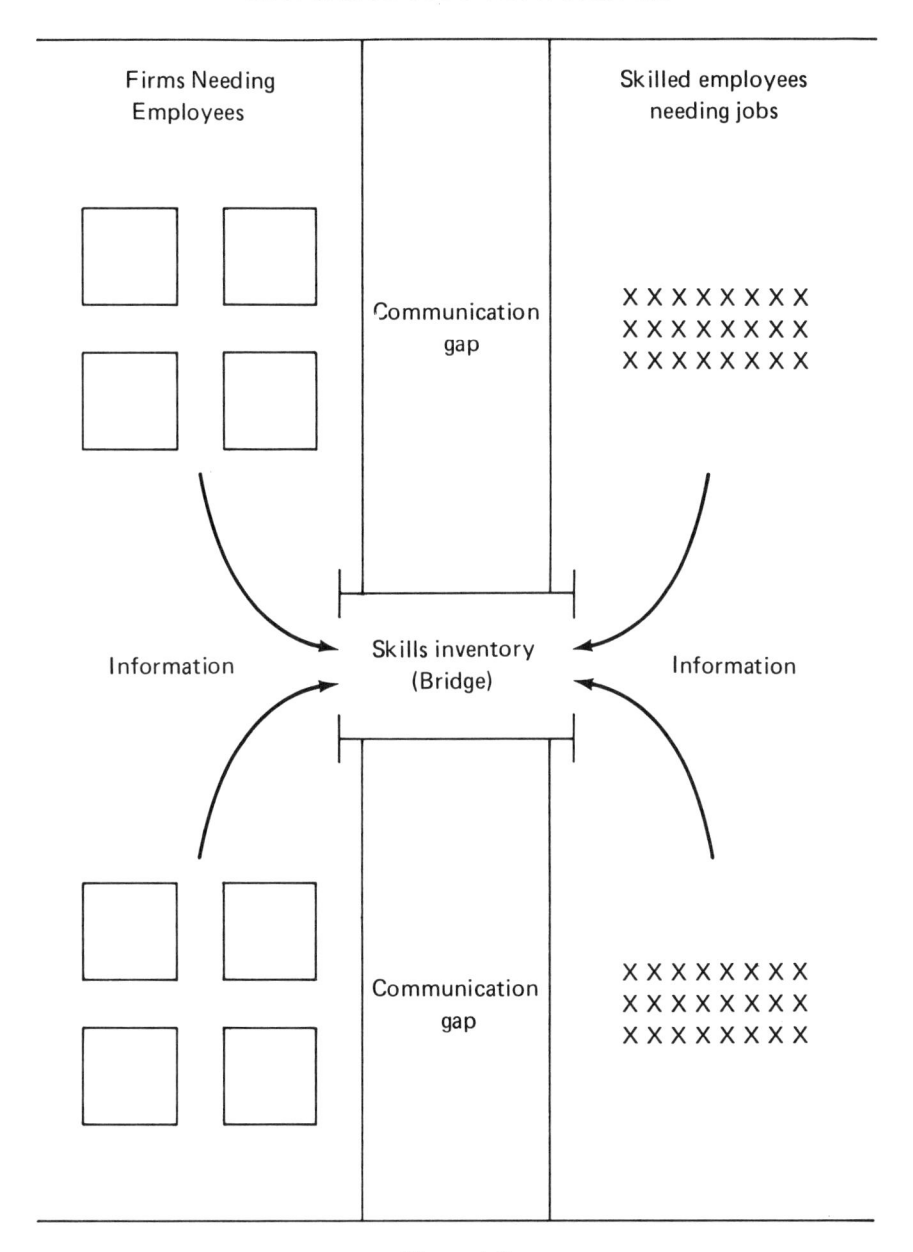

Figure 1-8

ticipation in decisions that have an impact on the employees themselves.

CENTRAL DATA BANK CONCEPT

Taking the concept of inventories a step further, it can be seen that there is the potential for reducing unemployment throughout the nation. Everyday, jobs are available, and people with the skills to do the work are unemployed and seeking work. Why could not the two be matched? At present, they are unaware of each other's existence. The organizations needing people suffer, and people looking for, but not finding the jobs suffer (Figure 1.8). This is truly a waste of our human resources.

The concept of a central data bank is technically feasible and some cities have experimented with it. The question on the other side of the coin is, do we want to? Centralization of information on any group of people has the possibility for abuse as well as for benefit. The damage done by erroneous credit and arrest records are but a few of the many examples available. These abuses have brought on the requirements for various disclosure laws including the Freedom of Information Act.

The potential benefits of having a universal inventory and maximizing our human resource potential is very tempting, but potential for misuse and abuse always looms threateningly on the horizon. If we could control the negative side, the potential for benefit is almost unlimited.

2
PARTS OF A CLASSICAL SYSTEM

PRIMARY INVENTORY SECTION

The classical skills inventory is generally composed of relatively predictable parts. These include the key words, work history, foreign languages, formal education, special courses, special projects, and vocational licenses. These are basic components found in most inventory systems (See Figure 2.1).

Key words are the heart of the system and will be reviewed in depth in a later section. These are the identifiers that separate the basic field, specialty and functions of jobs (See Figure 2.2). Key words are the terms that separate the marketing specialist from the accountant. They also provide a breakdown within a given area, such as accounting, to isolate the various types of accountants.

WORK HISTORY

Most inventories include a section on work history. This area provides two important sources of information. First, it gives us a method to identify the amount of experience a person really has and whether expertise really exists. In filling out inventory forms most people will not falsify information; however, there is always the human tendency to exaggerate. In this case, an item of experience of only six weeks may be listed as well as one of six years. Normally, requesting the person completing the form to indicate the time period involved will control this. Either the person will voluntarily exclude short time periods, or the system can readily identify and exclude them if desired.

BASIC COMPONENTS

Key words

\+

Work history

\+

Foreign languages

\+

Formal education

\+

Special courses

\+

Special projects

\+

Vocational license

———————

Total = Basic system

Figure 2-1

Parts of a Classical System 21

IDENTIFIERS
FIELDS AND SPECIALTIES

Personnel
1. Employment
2. Employee relations
3. Compensation
4. Benefits
5. Training
6. Etc.

Accounting
1. Cost accounting
2. Auditing
3. General ledger
4. Financial systems
5. Budgets
6. Etc.

KEY WORDS
(The heart of the system)

Marketing
1. Advertising
2. Creative arts
3. Sales promotion
4. Market information
5. Research
6. Etc.

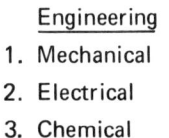

Engineering
1. Mechanical
2. Electrical
3. Chemical
4. Civil
5. Industrial
6. Etc.

Figure 2-2

The second reason involves work experience of a given mix or length. In the past, this determination has been largely intuitive, based on the supervisor or individual conducting the search. Recently, affirmative action criteria have challenged the validity and composition of the work "experience." Most jobs require that specific experience must also have supporting detailed job specifications which validate the required experience indicated. It is felt that work experience will continue to be a future item of significance, since many areas of work have legitimate experience requirements.

FOREIGN LANGUAGE

Foreign languages have always been included as part of skills inventory systems. Continued increase in international trade and activity has affected all firms large enough to use an inventory system (See Figure 2.3). At some time or another the situation arises (with increasing frequency) where a firm will require a document to be translated or someone to act as an interpreter in dealing with a customer. These requirements are business related and may involve substantial contracts and potential profits. This type of activity always gets the attention of management.

Inclusion of foreign language in a skills inventory is a relatively easy matter. The number of common spoken and written languages in which business is conducted is relatively small. The only other consideration is establishing proficiency levels such as the ability to read, write, speak, or the related combinations. This is also a minor coding situation and the entire language capability requires a relatively small amount of space in the inventory package.

The limited size and control of detail in language searches allow a very high degree of accuracy. The judgement factor in this category has been reduced to the point where language searches deliver a list of fully qualified employees. If contracts and profits are involved, and being able to communicate in a foreign language is a requirement, this area with its high degree of accuracy gives the entire inventory system a good name. Management is usually both pleased and complimentary when a system can deliver dollar generating accuracy.

USES OF CLASSICAL IDENTIFIERS

Item	Types of Uses
Key words	Separate fields, specialties and functions
Work history	Identifies amount of experience and the mix of experience
Foreign languages	Used to translate documents and identify interpreters
Formal education	May be a selection consideration—becoming less important with time
Special courses	Identify current knowledge and "state-of-the-art" knowledge
Special projects	Identify specific knowledge or experience acquired by work experience
Vocational licenses	Identify a certified unique skill

Figure 2-3

FORMAL EDUCATION

Formal education is an area that used to be one of the prime search targets or criteria, but it is currently decreasing in importance. The reasons for this decrease in importance are varied. Education, at least formal education, has not been able to keep pace with the changes in business and industry. Formal training in accounting, marketing, or other fields, if it is not coupled with current work experience soon makes the person obsolete. There are so many new developments each year that a person has to be working in a specified area to have "state of the art" knowledge.

In the past, a person trained for a career and this became his/her life's work. It was a rarity worthy of note to find someone working outside a formal career field for which they had completed training. Our changes in technology have blurred some career fields and brought obsolescence to others. It is commonplace today for a person to have a degree in one field and be working in a totally unrelated area. Also, where a person is working in his/her career field it is common for the individual to have moved into an administrative area or into a narrow area of specialization that has taken him/her out of the mainstream. Coupled with this is the continuing criterion that the parameters be job related. More and more, formal education becomes a factor not necessarily job related.

SPECIAL COURSES

Another item in the educational area seems to be filling part of the void. Those inventories that have an area to list special courses are finding increased activity. Many people are involved in the continuing education process, since it allows them to keep up (or catch up) in areas where technology has created a gap.

This area is also becoming of increasing importance to managers, since it gives them insight into who has some knowledge of a new or changed technology. A good example of the importance of this occurred back in the 1960s with the advent of computer technology. Few schools or colleges offered a degree in computer science or related fields. Consequently, the standard major and minor gave no indication of a person's knowledge of, or exposure to computers. A person might have substantial skills with computers, and have majors anywhere from history to psychology to electrical engineering or nuclear physics.

Most people were getting their computer education in one of two ways. First, by going back to formal institutions and taking the new courses as they were being offered. The second was through company or vendor sponsored courses coupled with on-the-job training. In both cases, this did not appear through the formal major/minor or degree which was normally used to search for a related educational background. This experience or training would only be reflected in the area of special courses designed to reflect internal or external training.

The entire concept of adult or continuing education and training is on the increase both within firms and in educational institutions. Rapid changes and advances in all fields are motivating people to return to the classrooms. Academic obsolescence is occurring at an ever-increasing rate.

SPECIAL PROJECTS

The use of projects as a search category for skills inventories quite possibly originated from aerospace or the military. Here many firms may have been involved in projects such as Apollo, Saturn, Mercury, etc. Information and knowledge gleaned from one firm or project could have direct application to another firm or follow-on project. Those individuals who had participated in earlier special projects were sought for the specific knowledge and experience they had developed.

Business firms in general have found that they now deal with large projects that cut across product line and industrial boundaries. Examples of these might be electronic data processing (EDP) system conversions, microfilm applications, skills inventory systems, etc. Those having experience on any one of these projects are definitely going to be of value to a firm working on the same item. Not only is the learning and orientation time reduced for the employee involved, but very valuable experience from previous exposure may also be involved.

This area may have greater future potential due to a management technique which is established in the manufacturing area and is increasing in popularity in other areas. This is the concept of project management which is becoming a popular tool. The basis of project management is to form a group with the necessary skills to accomplish a specific project. When the project is completed the group is dissolved and the staff goes on to other projects or returns to the formal organization.

There are several advantages to the project management structure. The group is dissolved when the project is completed, and this results in certain cost savings. The project concept enables you to cut across the formal organization lines to accomplish a task or solve a problem. This is becoming of ever-increasing importance as the complexity of change blurs formal organization lines. It is currently important to look at the whole rather than piece parts as formal organization structure dictates.

The use of projects on skills inventories has been of limited value in the past, and generally restricted to selected industries. Today this concept seems to be changing with the spread in business of the use of related projects, and with the increase of project management. Those developing inventories may want to give this area careful consideration.

VOCATIONAL LICENSES

Vocational licenses vary both in use and importance. However, when used they are of sufficient significance to be a major item in the inventory package. Normally, these licenses are state controlled, and lists are available from state government sources.

Searches in this area can be useful when looking for a unique skill such as that of landscape architect or nurseryman. It is an important source if a firm is building new sites or conducting remodeling and desires the use of internal advice or consulting. At the same time, this is an active source for internal searches in normal work functions such as those of an attorney or a CPA. In either case, the use of this category is normally sufficient to make this a major search category.

SECONDARY SEARCH CRITERIA

There are other items that can be found in skills inventories that are valuable, but are not in universal use or are found in relatively few companies. These are generally needed due to the unique nature of the firm, its product line, or the interests of key management personnel. These items, because of their relatively limited use, are grouped into the secondary category. Though they are listed in this grouping, they may be of prime importance to the firm or company involved.

Some of the traditional skills inventory items in this category are hobbies, social clubs, speaking clubs, publications, etc. There are many and varied applications of these items. An engineering company might find work related items by review of an individual's hobbies or publications. By the same token, a consulting or public relations firm, heavily engaged in public contact, might find social clubs and speaking clubs of paramount importance.

SELECTING PARTS OF THE INVENTORY

We know the uses of the classical identifiers used in a skills inventory (See Figure 2.3). How do we select the exact primary and secondary parts that should be used in banking rather than engineering? We know that banking people are involved in activities related to the financial world. This gives us an insight into the items that might be considered in the key word lists as well as those dealing with work experience, education and special courses. For international banking we would also assume that language proficiency has definite value.

Other primary areas might create some problems in preparing lists specifically for banking. Professional memberships might vary by location, as might the specific inventory items of "Location Preference." Items to be included in "Vocational Licenses" and "Position Preferences" would probably be determined by the size and structure of the banking organization. Even in the lists of primary items there is still significant review and consideration involved before a final list of acceptable inventory criteria is established.

Assuming that, as with any industry, the primary group will be included for banking, the difficulty in developing lists for the categories can be seen. We know we want the categories, but exactly what will go into them may not be readily apparent.

Further, what about such secondary items as hobbies, social clubs, speaking clubs, publications? Here we are not just determining what goes onto a list, but whether we want to use an entire category or not. In fact, in the secondary area we have to consider whether we have even thought of all the possible areas of categories that might be applicable.

We need an approach to developing lists for the primary categories, and to establishing both categories and related lists for the secondary categories. One approach to this problem, which has worked in the past, is to use existing managers and supervisors for input and screening of the lists and categories. What is needed is a determination of what lists go in each category. Most people familiar with the organization can draft an initial list which is then circulated to concerned managers and supervisors for additions. Since an initial list has been provided, the response is usually rapid and productive. As with any other activity, all the experts reveal themselves once something has been put in writing.

Establishing both the categories and related lists would work similarly for the secondary items. A tentative group would be prepared and circulated to involved managers and supervisors. Their comments, suggestions and additions would then be included and recirculated. This modified Delphi method is excellent for obtaining input which coincides with what the firm or company needs and can work with.

Too often inventories have been designed and used across the board, and they do not reflect what a company needs or wants. Each company has individual characteristics and requirements. To be truly successful a skills inventory must take these into consideration. An inventory that meets the needs and requirements for engineering will not necessarily do so for banking. In fact, within banking, those inventories meeting the needs of large banks may not do so for small and medium sized ones.

AREAS OF GREATEST SIGNIFICANCE

Under normal circumstances those items in the primary category are most actively searched. The specific category or combination of categories will be selected based on the type of search or specific ability that is being sought. This may vary over a period of time as requirements within the operation change.

The most frequently targeted areas for searches are those related to job openings. This would probably include the categories of "key words" and job "experience," since these are directly job related items. It is not uncommon to add education or special courses, or to include other factors that might reduce the population chosen or include additional skills.

The foreign language category might be searched directly if someone is being sought to translate a document or interpret a conversation. It also might be an adjunct to a job opening search for someone needed in a foreign country or a neighborhood where a particular language is spoken. This area, as indicated earlier, is expanding due to the increase in international activity.

The categories related to education may also be searched individually. These are frequently used for survey participation. Many salary surveys as well as internal research projects focus heavily on degree, major, etc.

Those categories remaining are normally used for a specific need or project as they occur. This same concept applies to the secondary categories. In fact, each must be examined and used, based on the specific needs and requirements of the group or groups requesting the inventory search.

3
KEY WORDS
THE HEART OF THE SYSTEM

DEFINITION OF KEY WORDS

It was earlier stated that we would go into the definition of key words in depth. The term, key words, indicates a significant ranking—being a cut above the other identifiers used. When searching for a specific work skill these are the categories most often referred to. This is the group of words or identifiers that separates the accountant from the marketing specialist, then further separates the tax accountant from the cost accountant, and may break the tax accountant into various sub-groups.

One of the best ways to understand the functions of key words is to think of the classified section of a newspaper, in particular the help wanted section where job openings are listed. Here an attempt is made to index jobs on a rough key word basis. The words, attempt, and, rough, should be emphasized here. Most newspaper advertisements do not approach the degree of definition key word indexes should have. They wind up as more of a straight alphabetical listing, but some do make an effort at a first or major identifier level.

Assume, for instance, that you are in the area of personnel. In most classified job listings this is where you will find those jobs in the area dealing with the major topic of personnel. This will probably contain perhaps only ninety percent of the personnel related jobs. The remainder will be found under other headings such as industrial relations or human resource management. Some will be further buried within an advertisement under a company or organization's name where all of their job openings are listed together. If you read any of the books describing job hunting you will find many suggest you look over the entire classified section, and not just search under your particular area. This suggestion helps by locating those jobs in your area that would otherwise be buried.

Now, looking at the approximately ninety percent or so actually listed under personnel in the newspaper there may or may not be an attempt to provide further order. There are many second level breakdowns within personnel. Examples would be employment, compensation, benefits, employee relations, training, etc. In some cases there is an effort to keep all employment type jobs together, all compensation jobs in groups, and so on.

Most efforts at this type of grouping also seem to fail. Employment type jobs might fall into many different categories such as recruiter, employment specialist, interviewer, executive recruitment, and many others. Those looking for jobs in the employment area may also find them under a specific company listing in the personnel section, which also may be looking for compensation analysts and claim processors. In other words, even in the personnel sections a person would have to review the entire section to find all of the openings that he/she might be interested in or qualified for.

THE HEART OF THE SYSTEM

The above problems give some insight into why the key words are the heart of the system. If properly set up and organized you should be able to go directly to the areas that identify the skill being sought. A properly designed key word system can save a great deal of time and money.

It must be remembered, that we will be asking the employees to search through a set of instructions and to identify themselves. They are not going to have the same motivation as they would have in searching the classified ads for a job. People under pressure for a job willingly take their own time and review the paper from cover to cover. Those completing the skills inventory form are not under that type of pressure. Also, we may be allowing them to complete the inventory on company time. Management does not want hours spent reviewing lists for various alternate words that have the same meaning.

By the same token, organizations using skills inventories want to be able to store and retrieve the data that is submitted. We want to be able to go directly to a specific area and find those with the skills we are looking for. It is desirable to do this work with as few identifiers as possible. The last thing that is wanted is to have to wander over the entire file in a random manner, and then not even be assured that all those qualified have been identified.

Using computer technology has probably forced us to take an even more serious look at structuring key words. The computer acts only on the instructions provided, and these must have a logical base. However, the cost factors involved may be an even stronger motivation. If we make a retrieval and do not get the necessary information, we still pay a price in both our time and machine time. This, of course, can compound as multiple searches are made with little or no results. Hence, proper structuring of the key word system is of paramount importance.

STRUCTURING OF THE KEY WORD SYSTEM

An effective way to approach the structuring of a key word system is to do it in levels or layers, going from the general to the more specific. When someone is asked what he/she does for a living, very often the response is to give the major area we work in, such as "Engineer." If someone pursues the question further, we tend to go to the next level, say to an "Electrical Engineer," and generally the name of the firm or organization is mentioned either in step one or two.

We have become used to a certain leveling system in common social conversation. Few people enter any greater depths than to give the general type of work and the organization where they work. The exception to this occurs when someone is applying for a job. Here the general category and type of organization are used as a screening device. They serve to let the initial interviewer know which technical specialist to refer the applicant to for further questioning. It is very possible that this initial interviewer will go through several levels to be certain where the applicant fits.

This same concept of leveling has a direct application to our key word structuring. Most of us tend to put ourselves into a broad category of work or skill. For our purposes here, let us refer to this broad area as the major identifier (See Figure 3.1). This then goes another step to what we shall refer to as the second level which is a more specific definition of one's skills. This second level can be seen in Figure 3.1. We may also hear people refer to this socially as their area of work, if they are questioned further about their occupations.

In Figure 3.2 we have a third level of skill. Taken together with the major identifier and second level we have a fairly good idea of what the person is proficient at, or what his/her area of specialization may be.

There are various ways to continue this concept of leveling for even greater insight into the person's specialty. One way is to add a verb which describes the function that the individual performs. An employee may be analyzing, estimating, interviewing, instructing, counseling, writing, planning, etc. This gives a much broader picture of the person's skills background.

Figure 3.3 shows this verb modifier used with just the major identifiers and the second level of skill. This gives a better picture of how the skill is being used. Some systems might allow for more than one, or multiple verb modifiers on the same function. For example a person may be both supervising and analyzing the same function. Someone might be teaching, counseling, and writing to effectively perform a given function.

We can even take the concept of leveling a step further (See Figure 3.4). Here we have combined the verb modifiers with the major level through to the third level identifiers. This provides even more visibility for those using the system, and greater opportunity for the employees to express themselves. Here an employee can show he/she is supervising a cost accounting operation or analyzing a general accounting function.

This verb concept can be very useful when actually conducting a search, particularly in a large firm. Assume that we have several hundred people doing general accounting work. Our requirement is

MAJOR AND SECOND LEVEL IDENTIFIERS
Examples

Major Identifiers	Second Level
Business administration	Accounting
	Personnel
	Management
	Marketing
Engineering	Aeronautical
	Civil
	Electrical
	Industrial
	Marine
	Mechanical
	Nuclear

Figure 3-1

MAJOR THROUGH THIRD LEVEL IDENTIFIERS

Examples

Major Identifiers	Second Level	Third Level
Business administration	Accounting	Cost accounting
		General accounting
		Tax accounting
	Personnel	Benefits
		Compensation
		Employment
		Employee relations
		Training

Figure 3-2

MAJOR AND SECOND LEVEL IDENTIFIERS
WITH
VERB MODIFIERS

Examples

Major Identifiers	Second Level	Verb Modifiers
Business administration	Accounting	Analyzing
	Personnel	Counseling
	Management	Planning
	Marketing	Supervising
Engineering	Aeronautical	Analyzing
	Civil	Supervising
	Electrical	Supervising
	Industrial	Analyzing
	Marine	Estimating
	Mechanical	Estimating
	Nuclear	Supervising

Figure 3-3

MAJOR THROUGH THIRD LEVEL IDENTIFIERS
WITH
VERB MODIFIERS

Examples

Major Identifers	Second Level	Third Level	Verb Modifers
Business administration	Accounting	Cost accounting	Supervising
		General accounting	Analyzing
		Tax accounting	Supervising
	Personnel	Benefits	Analyzing
		Compensation	Planning
		Employment	Interviewing
		Employee relations	Counseling
		Training	Instructing

Figure 3-4

for a position requiring supervisory experience in the field. Selecting from those who have a cost accounting background and who show supervising in the verb modifier area gives us this visibility.

The question arises as to how many levels are enough, or what are the optimum number of levels. This most often seems to be dictated by the number of functions (See Figure 3.5). In fact, the number of functions can be more important than the size of a firm or organization. A highly technical area that contains many and varied functions would be a candidate for multiple levels. At the same time, a large firm with mostly manufacturing of a limited nature, that had neither large research and development nor diversified engineering function might have few levels.

SPACE ALLOCATION FOR KEY WORDS

It must be kept in mind that many people will have more than one set of key words. Particularly today, people change fields and specialities often. It is this very fact that is the basis for establishing skills inventories. The skills that are not commonly known about, or readily apparent, can be the very ones we are most interested in locating and identifying.

There is no specific rule for the amount of space that will be set aside to identify the key words. If we assume that a line would include all the levels determined necessary for that organization, we might establish some rough guidelines. Most people should be allowed to display themselves in at least three lines of three separate skill areas. It would be rare to find someone with experience today who did not have at least this many skills in his/her background. Many organizations allow for more than the minimum, and often you will see systems that allow a dozen or more.

If you severely restrict the number you force the employee to do the editing. This may or may not be desirable. Most employees are conditioned by society to complete forms in chronological order. A skills inventory form closely resembles the job application, which usually carries with it the threat of job loss for falsification.

If the number of lines to display one's skills is limited, this can

Key Words—The Heart of the System 39

FUNCTIONS VERSUS IDENTIFIERS

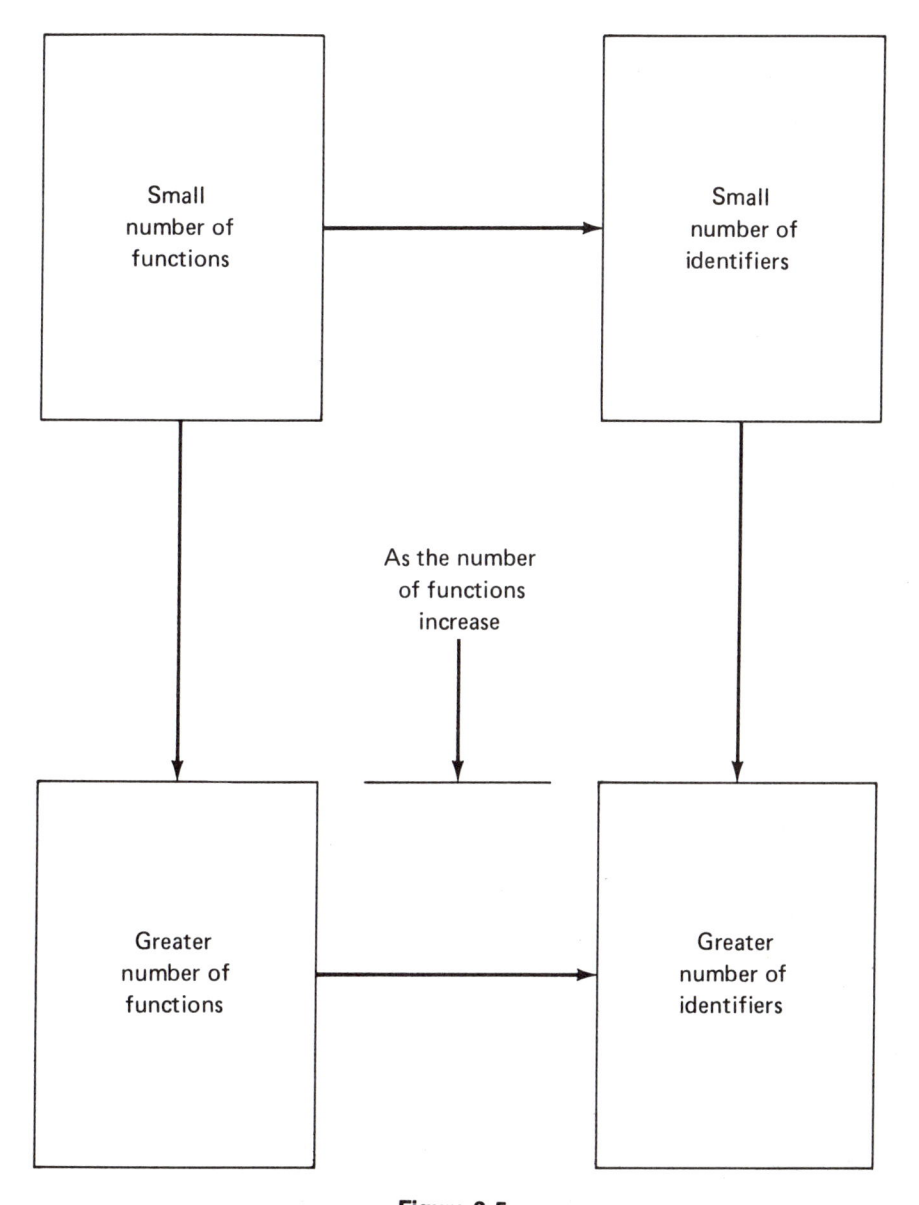

```
┌─────────────┐                    ┌─────────────┐
│   Small     │                    │   Small     │
│  number of  │──────────────────▶ │  number of  │
│  functions  │                    │ identifiers │
└──────┬──────┘                    └──────┬──────┘
       │                                  │
       │         As the number            │
       │          of functions            │
       │           increase               │
       │              │                   │
       ▼              ▼                   ▼
┌─────────────┐                    ┌─────────────┐
│   Greater   │                    │   Greater   │
│  number of  │──────────────────▶ │  number of  │
│  functions  │                    │ identifiers │
└─────────────┘                    └─────────────┘
```

Figure 3-5

create a problem. Employees may put down their last several areas out of routine form completion patterns. What we are looking for are those skills that are most significant and in which the employee is strongest or most proficient. If the number of lines is limited the instructions should be very clear on what is sought. The employee should be encouraged to skip limited or inconsequential skill areas and focus on those of the greatest importance and significance.

Space should also be provided so that the amount of time in months or years a person has performed a specific skill can be shown. Time can be an important factor in evaluating proficiency, for this allows a screening out of those people who have had only a brief encounter with a particular skill. If the years are shown rather than just the number of months, we have some additional visibility as to how current the skill is. As the rapid change in advancement and technology takes place, the concern for current or up-to-date knowledge becomes a more significant factor.

NEED TO MEET UNIQUE ORGANIZATIONAL REQUIREMENTS

The key words, if at all possible, should be tied to the language used within the specific organization involved. Too many inventories start out with a key word index that is a copy of that used by some other organization. Often the words are not familiar, or there are a number of terms that do not apply to the organization adopting the list.

Each organization has its special language. An inventory is most effective when it uses that language. Nothing is more frustrating than for aerospace engineers to have to plow through lists of forest products or canning industry terms to identify themselves. By the same token the reverse is also true for those in forest products or the canning industry.

The same thing applies for the coding that may be used on the key words, particularly, if the data is being entered into an automated system, the key words are assigned a code to reduce the storage space and speed up the entry and retrieval. This code may be alpha or numeric (e.g. 0011 or AC may stand for accounting). Similar coding systems may also exist in the organization for systems other than the skills inventory.

These other coding systems should be reviewed very carefully. Chances are good that if they have been in existence for any period of time the organization is both comfortable and familiar with them. It is possible that after review, parts of these may be applicable to the skills inventory. Being able to adopt these can make acceptance of the inventory easier, as well as cutting down on training and familarization time.

Prior to implementing any key word or coding system, it is suggested that these be carefully reviewed within the organization. Copies should be sent to major department heads. They should be asked to review the system for accuracy and completeness. In addition, they should be asked to indicate those areas listed that are not applicable.

There may be some conflicts or differences of opinion on what to add or to delete. One department manager may wish to expand one of the key word categories, while another may wish it to be deleted. These are significant issues which we want to surface early.

Remember, these key words are the heart of the system. It is imperative that all problems and disagreements be resolved as best as possible before the inventory is implemented throughout the organization. Problems of terminology can be handled much easier before the system is fully operational. To accomplish a review and some level of consensus, it may take several revisions of the initial key word structure and related coding. On areas of strong disagreement, it may take a number of meetings to iron out the difficulties. However, all of this activity will be worth it in the long run.

KEY WORDS AND THE REQUISITION SYSTEM

When considering which key word system will be used, it is best to keep in mind the existing requisition system—that is to say the forms and/or procedures used to hire or transfer people into an open job. Ideally, we want to tie the skills inventory directly to the requisition system. All open requisitions, or job openings, may also be tested against the skills inventory system for possible candidates.

To achieve this end we want to insure, if possible, that the two systems are compatible. This will be discussed in more detail in a later chapter, but its significance must be noted here. It is worthwhile considerating the inclusion of the key words as part of the requisition system. When management wishes to replace someone, they ask for them using the key word system.

This strengthens the skills inventory concept in several ways. It aids management in becoming thoroughly familiar with the key words, and it allows the skills inventory to be used on all open requisitions. This in turn creates employee interest and participation. There is more willingness on everyone's part to participate in the skills inventory, if it is known all openings are to be tested against it.

4
INVENTORY INPUT FORMS

INPUT FORMS

Every system requires input, or a method for the information to be fed in initially, and then updated as changes occur. Not only is this true with skills inventory systems, but it is made even more complex since we are dealing with people. Each person is submitting data on his/her background. While the system requires standard input, each person strives to detail his/her own unique qualities.

This autobiographical information may tend to vary slightly, since no two people have the same identical backgrounds. Depending on the structure of the system and the number of categories, the number of totally identical duplications may be very small. This means that most people will have unique information, but hopefully it will be identical or very close for groupings of people within selected categories. This is the basis for being able to perform an inventory search. It is this area of standardization which allows the system to work.

In any event, capturing the information on individuals is always the first step. Following this, and just as important, is the maintenance and updating of the information. We will therefore need a system to make corrections or changes. The initial input form or procedure can be designed to perform this function as well. Doing this in a single step avoids duplication and allows for savings in both time and money. It also simplifies the procedure, so we do not have to look for different sets of input documents.

INFORMATION-GATHERING PROBLEMS

There are many ways to obtain data about people. One of the more common ways is to have each person fill out a form. If the questions are simple and to the point, this can go with relative smoothness. The problem in the skills inventory area is that the questions we would like to ask are neither simple nor to the point. Usually, we are seeking a large amount of information for an adequate data file for search purposes. We are seeking to build a file of rather complex data and background information to allow us wide search flexibility in the future.

Remember, we are asking people to identify fields, specialties, functions, etc. for tasks which they are able to perform. In essence, we are asking them to identify their various skills from lists or groups of possibilities. This brings into play a lot of psychological and actual operational problems in obtaining consistent and accurate input.

Some people tend to hold back or not identify all of the areas of capabilities that they have. This is especially true with the more experienced or professional types. There is a feeling that their reputations have been established through years of work and experience. They feel they no longer have to give the organization information and that they are above this type of requirement.

In small firms their assumption might be correct. This is not true, however, in the middle-size and large firms where skills inventories are most often used. Probably, only the top thirty to fifty people are totally visible throughout the organization. The remainder, though having some visibility, are blind spots for many areas of the organization. All of these people would benefit from the additional exposure which the skills inventory concept provides. Unfortunately, many people do not have this overview or broad perspective, and are concerned only with their immediate, and usually limited, career area.

The other side of the coin deals with those who tend to give too much information, and also, with those who tend to exaggerate. The term exaggerate seems appropriate, since few people actually lie when submitting inventory data. There is often the tendency to note some background items or skills they have dealt with, but for very limited time periods.

There are several reasons why those actually fabricating material are generally not a problem for skills inventory systems. Most organizations that are large enough to have and use inventories, generally screen applicants before hiring, and require that an application form be completed. Large portions of this information is normally verified. Those people submitting false data are usually caught before being hired, or within a short period of time after they have been hired. Remember, a skills inventory is generally completed after the hiring process.

Most people working for a company have generally provided it with a great deal of information about themselves. Included in this would be such items as, the application, performance evaluations, educational changes, etc. Employees generally are hesitant about noting anything that might be at variance with any information they have previously supplied. Even if they would like to falsify information, there is a tendency not to, since they know or believe that the organization already has this information about them.

Finally, most areas have their inventories either controlled directly, or routed through the personnel department. Most personnel departments, particularly those large enough to use skills inventories, have an employee record section and maintain a master personnel file on employees. Most companies also have strict rules about falsification of records, violation of which normally results in discharge.

Because of this threat, most people view the sending of incorrect or false information to the personnel department as a dangerous undertaking. In fact, it seems that everyone is certain (sometimes to the point of being paranoid) that all records and data are cross-checked to seek out anyone who deliberately makes an incorrect statement. In actuality very little cross-checking generally occurs after a person has been hired; however, this image acts as a strong deterrent to those who might be tempted to stray from the truth.

It was noted earlier that though very few people actually lie, there will be some who will exaggerate. Instances will occur where staff members show items of work experience, key word identifiers, etc., for tasks that they have been involved with for only a few weeks or months—enough time to give them exposure, but not enough time to achieve anything approaching proficiency.

This is often noted with participants in management training programs. Many times, there is exposure over a very short period of time to major functions in all areas. If this same data is transferred to the skills biography in the key word or work history area, it can give an exaggerated though not a false appearance (See Figure 4.1).

A suggestion for avoiding this problem is to include a specific skills inventory item. Knowing that someone worked in marketing or performed an accounting task for less than one month is important. It is particularly important if we are looking for someone with the proficiency that only five or ten years on the job can bring. Having a time factor included allows us the option of sorting or selecting on this factor. In this way we can let the "eager beavers" display themselves in any category they choose without concern. We can always screen out or limit our candidate lists to those with a certain level of required experience.

There is also the option of limiting the entries on the system to those of a given length of time. For example, it can be stated as a part of the instructions that "six months experience" with a given factor must be achieved before it can be included. This solves part of the problem, but creates another. It would tend to discourage or sour the young and eager employee who does not have a great deal of experience. This is the same person who may be part of the future management team, and the one we want most to use and support the system in the future. It may be much easier to let this person put down all of his/her experience, regardless of how short a duration. If a time factor showing how long a person performed a given task or function is included, we can maintain control and screen accordingly. At the same time, good management/employee relations are fully preserved.

IDEAL INFORMATION COLLECTION

There are many methods of collecting information on people. These range from the expert collecting, analyzing and submitting the data,

FACTUAL BUT EXAGGERATED SKILLS INVENTORY DATA

Samples of input from someone spending only six weeks in a manufacturing training program. Note how the data on work experience can be misinterpreted without a time factor.

1. *Without a time factor:*

    Work Experience

    Production Control

    Engineering

    General Manufacturing

2. *With a time factor:*

Work experience	Length of time
Production Control	2 weeks
Engineering	2 weeks
General Manufacturing	2 weeks

Figure 4-1

to the person performing this function him/herself. The most effective and accurate method is to have this done by an expert, however, as with most systems, we pay a premium for the ideal system.

Let us look at what we might consider to be the ideal collection system. We indicated that an expert would be involved. This expert might be someone who is experienced in in-depth interviewing techniques. In the ideal situation our experienced interviewer would work with the employee reviewing each category in the skills inventory system in detail.

The interviewer would ask the appropriate questions and obtain the most accurate answers for each category in the inventory. At the same time the employee would have a chance to ask questions regarding the meaning of unclear terms, purpose, use, etc., which deal with any or all aspects of the organization's system. In the ideal system the expert may actually complete the input forms involved. The employee would act as a verbal data source supplying the information needed to complete his/her inventory background. Again, any questions or concerns could be explored to the satisfaction of both the interviewer and the employee. At the completion of the interview, the employee could review and sign the input sheet which the interviewer had prepared, and so satisfy those concerned with security and accuracy.

As with training, a one-on-one teaching/learning experience can be very beneficial, but the costs are very high. In the previous example we have the employee's time and the cost of the interviewer. Stop and think of the many hours even an experienced manager has to take to interview someone for a position. Sometimes the interview is completed in a shorter period of time, but this may vary, and it is best to schedule accordingly. Someone being interviewed who has many questions can greatly extend the time involved.

The same situation can occur in the skills inventory interviewing process. We cannot completely control the time involved without reducing the involvement of the employee and his/her opportunity to ask questions. If we do this, we may have lost the goodwill and the important desire to participate. The cost in this instance in staff hours can be significant.

EMPLOYEE COMPLETION

The other end of the spectrum from the interviewer-assisted completion is a skills inventory which is designed for completion by the employee alone. There is no interviewer, and except for special questions no second person is involved. Each employee reads the instructions and prepares the input form individually. Normally, there are routing or mailing instructions included so that the form can be directed to the appropriate area for input to the system when completed.

For obvious reasons many firms use, or attempt to use, variations of this concept. The cost is greatly reduced because only one person instead of two is involved in completing the form. There is flexibility, since the employee does not have to be at a specific place at a certain time for the form to be completed. In fact, since only the employee is involved, the completion may be spread over a period of time, with one part being completed when convenient, and another part completed later should interruptions occur. This method also makes the situation much easier to handle for firms that have geographically dispersed locations and groups of people.

Many times skills inventories are used for the salaried or professional person. The time loss here can be even less than for the hourly or blue collar worker. Professional people, by the nature and definition of their work, are paid to perform a specific function or set of functions. They are paid for performing, rather than for the hours that are put in. If they take a half hour to two hours to complete the form, productivity is not necessarily reduced. Most professional employees are going to get their work done even if it means staying late, taking work home, or coming in early. It is this type of behavior that aids in making them a separate and distinct group.

It is also a reality that due to a variety of reasons, including the personal and confidential nature of skills inventory information, that the inventory may be the item that is taken home for completion. Thus a minimal amount of time is lost.

A package that is to be completed by an employee will be somewhat different in structure from one to be completed with assistance. The secret here lies in the clarity of the instructions and examples provided. It boils down to a complex exercise in written communication. If one is planning on using such a system on a sizable group, it should be field tested on all levels within an organization prior to implementation. Nothing can be more embarrassing or costly, than to send out a package to be completed by hundreds or thousands of people which is not clear and fully understandable. It is also one of the easiest problems to avoid.

One has but to identify those types that will be involved and pilot test the package with representative sample groups, and directly solicit their responses on which areas are unclear or need further explanation. People are always ready to provide criticism without much pushing. This becomes even more so if you give them something in writing, as this becomes an official and concrete target. By using this resource constructively we can iron out most of the major difficulties before going into mass production. One pilot testing series may not be enough. It may take two, three, or more until all the major problems and misunderstandings have been changed and cleared up. Spending the time at this stage prevents a lot of grief in the future.

BETWEEN THE IDEAL AND EMPLOYEE COMPLETION

As with any other activity, it would be difficult to find either extreme in its pure form (See Figure 4.2). Most organizations tend more toward the "employee completion" concept, if for no other reason than because it keeps costs under control. At the same time, most organizations, the same as most individuals, toy with ideal concepts. Part of the reason for this may be that technological advances continue to make fantasies realities in today's world.

Where the "employee completion" concept is practiced, we will also find many modifications practiced within the same organization. Senior employees, out of courtesy, are often provided with one-on-one assistance in completing their forms. This continues to ensure that their time is maximized and not spent unnecessarily reviewing instructions. By the same token, managers and supervisors may

IDEAL SYSTEM VERSUS EMPLOYEE COMPLETION

	Time to Complete	Instruction Package	Form Design	Overall Cost of System
IDEAL SYSTEM	COST <u>HIGH</u> (2 people involved at firm's expense) CONTINUING COST	COST <u>LOW</u> (Handled by interviewer) ONE-TIME COST	COST <u>LOW</u> (Interviewer there to complete) ONE-TIME COST	COST <u>HIGH</u> (Time of 2 people offsets other savings) CONTINUING
EMPLOYEE COMPLETION	COST <u>LOW</u> (1 person involved, possibly on his/her own time) CONTINUING COST	COST <u>HIGH</u> (Must be designed so each individual can understand) ONE-TIME COST	COST <u>HIGH</u> (Must be designed so each individual can complete) ONE-TIME COST	COST <u>LOW</u> (Time of one person, possibly on his/her own time) CONTINUING

Figure 4-2

bring their groups together and complete the input documents in a joint effort during a staff meeting. This may aid in answering questions and in furthering understanding, but it also serves to negate cost savings by those who would complete the form in off hours at home.

DESIGNING THE FORM

The form used would tend to vary in complexity. An ideal situation where the form is either completed by, or with the assistance of a trained interviewer, would probably require less time in development. Here we would depend on the experience of the interviewer who would be completing the form on a frequent basis. The input form could be complex and the correct data would still be captured in a consistent and reliable manner.

The "employee completion" form is an entirely different matter. Here we expect the individual to complete the form by him/herself, and in most cases without assistance. The design of this type of form is critical. If it is not completed properly the necessary data will not be captured. Even worse, if the data is to be input to a computer and is not placed in exactly the appropriate sequence on the form, we can have major errors in our computer file. This in turn can create erroneous reports and subject the entire system to criticism.

As can readily be understood, the design and also the multiple testing on pilot groups is vital. The groups involved in the pilot testing should include employees from all segments of the organization involved. Only in this way can we insure that the form is functional and accurately captures the data from groups at all levels.

Many inventories and the related input forms are designed strictly for one group of people. For example, many inventories are designed primarily for salaried or professional employees. At a later date, it may be necessary to put all, or part, of the hourly employees into the system. Many times such a decision is dictated by union agreements or an Affirmative Action ruling. It may not be possible to expand the existing system, if the original input form and related instructions were not designed to be flexible.

It is important to have the input forms tested against all possible future users. Suppose we only plan to use the system on the salaried population. We know that adding part or all of our hourly population is always a possibility. Why not design the system for both groups, and test it on both groups? We may have to add some key words or other identifiers, but this certainly is not a total waste of space or time. We know that realistically part of our salary population came up through the ranks, and at one time had held hourly positions. These same key words should be included in our lists anyway for this group to identify itself. Remember, part of their background was as hourly employees and most people want to reflect all their experience and skills.

At the same time, we can be ready should we decide to add the hourly people at a later date. They can be included in the sample pilot tests. The skills inventory input forms and instructions can be designed to accommodate their inputs. From a systems point of view we have not painted ourselves into a corner. We have not designed a system that cannot be expanded without major systems revisions.

TURNAROUND FORMS

The proper design of forms can be a great help in making the form more clear for all those involved. Such a form is often referred to as a "turnaround" form (See Figure 4.3). This name comes from the fact that it is designed as both an input and output form.

Normally, we find turnaround forms used with an automated system. The form is designed so that the computer prints the current information directly on to the form. This is then sent to the appropriate person for review and any corrections or necessary changes can then be made in the space provided. Usually this blank space is placed right next to the corresponding computer printed data. An employee sees what information is on file and can make the necessary changes in the adjacent space provided. This form is then returned with the changes noted—hence, the term turnaround.

The value of using a turnaround is that you have two documents

TURNAROUND DOCUMENT

<u>Sample</u>

NAME: R. L. Jones		
DEPARTMENT: 68-00		
SOCIAL SECURITY NUMBER: XXX-XX-XXXX		
EDUCATION:		
Degree	Major	College
<u>Actual</u>		
1 B.S.	Bus. Admin.	U.C.L.A.
2		
<u>Correction/Change</u>		
1		
2		
LANGUAGES:		
Name		Proficiency
<u>Actual</u>		
1 French		Read
2 Spanish		Read and write
3		
<u>Correction/Change</u>		
1		
2		
3		

Figure 4-3

in one. Without it you have to have one form for input, and another for output. There is always the problem of locating and storing separate forms. One or the other always seems to be missing when needed most. This just adds to the complexity and slows the process of input and output.

5
INVENTORY STORAGE AND PROCESSING

TYPES OF STORAGE AND PROCESSING

The data is received through one input processing method or another as we discussed in the last chapter. The question is, what should be done with the large volume of material that has been gathered? We have to store it in some logical manner so that we can retrieve it at a future time.

Think of the skills inventory data as stock or inventory and the processing system as the warehouse and corresponding cataloguing system. Our stock or inventory cannot be placed in the warehouse in a random manner. Should this happen we could not readily locate an item when needed. The stock must be stored in a logical manner and catalogued in such a way that we know where to find it.

The same concept applies to skills inventory data. We want to store it logically and be able to readily retrieve it at some future date. When we are doing a search, it is usually because we have a problem for which we must find a solution. If we do not get the answer in a timely fashion the system is not meeting our needs. One of the main things we want to remember is that the response time of the system is critical.

It is often assumed that since we are dealing with data and the collection of data we must have a computer system to operate a skills inventory. This is a misconception that often discourages smaller units and companies from considering a skills inventory. They immediately envision a multimillion-dollar computer installation, sophisticated equipment and a large resident staff of technical experts. This notion is erroneous and many miss out on the benefits of the use of skills inventories because of it. In the next few pages we will discuss the use of manual systems, the classical computer-based system, and some other alternatives to investing in a major computer installation.

DECISIONS ON PROCESSING

The size of the particular firm or unit and the complexity of the probable skills available must be considered. For example, a small- to medium-sized manufacturing plant of five hundred to a thousand people would require a certain mix of skills to operate effectively. These skills would be somewhat limited and to a certain degree predictable.

Here, size directly correlates with the complexity of the skills and their mix. On the other hand, let us assume we have a firm of this size which is a "think tank" or a research and development facility. In this instance we have a group of scientists, engineers, technicians, etc. who, in many cases, have widely diverse backgrounds, experience, education. Almost every person possesses his/her individual area of expertise, with no two people having the same qualifications. Such a group might require a system complex enough to handle a large firm of relatively standard or average skills makeup.

Other considerations might include the existing processing capabilities that are available. The decision whether to use a computer or to use a manual system for processing inventory material depends upon the type of equipment that is readily available, and the projected growth in the organization's use of it. For example, let us assume that the firm is small in size with a relatively limited skill mix. Assume six hundred employees in a manufacturing industry, and assume that there is no existing computer system either within the firm or being used outside by it. Here we might want to seriously consider using a manual system.

Two questions arise. First, is there a "rule of thumb" for what size an organization should be to warrant a skills inventory system? The best answer to this is the limits of the computer or the human brain.

When we can no longer review and remember accurately the backgrounds and knowledge of employees, a skills inventory becomes a valuable asset. As we mentioned earlier, a manufacturing firm with standard skills might have around five hundred to one thousand employees while a "think tank" or research and development operation might have one hundred or even less. When the people who perform the personnel management functions have to start calling around for leads as to who has what type of skills, the time for an inventory system is *past due*.

Another question that frequently comes up is "when do we go from a manual system to a computer?" Again, we have to stop and evaluate our present capabilities and future plans. Do we have a computer or the use of computer time available? Is there a possibility that our system is going to grow substantially over a period of time? If we have access to a computer *and* we plan on growing, the manual processing consideration may not be one we want to pursue. On the other hand, if the organization is small, the skills mix is rather standard, we have no future plans for major expansion, and we do not have either a computer or access to computer time, we would probably want to go to a manual option.

By the same token, just having computer capability does not mean we will use it. Since there are very real costs involved in computer usage, a cost analysis is a must. The cost of using the computer must be offset by the benefits—tangible or intangible—which are received. This can sometimes be both the most important and the most difficult part of our decision.

MANUAL METHODS

There are all types of manual approaches to setting up a skills inventory. There are internally developed systems as well as different variations that are marketed by various firms. The best approach to setting up a manual system is to think about what we are storing and what we want to retrieve in the future. Basically, we have groupings of terms. There is work experience, key words, languages, etc. When we search the system we want to know who has which skills, education, or capabilities. We might also be looking for combinations of these.

One approach to setting up a manual skills inventory is to use a set of index cards similar to those you find at the local library. These can be arranged under several different skills categories in alphabetical order. One will probably be in key word order, since this will normally be a major area of search (See Figure 5.1). Another will be in alphabetical order of work experience (See Figure 5.2). These might also be cross-referenced to other items in the skills inventory such as education, special courses, etc.

These cards allow us to have a map reference to the system. When we search the cards and find candidates who meet our original search criteria, we can then refer to the employees' original biographies in the personnel folders. Here we can review other pertinent information regarding the individual or individuals we are seeking. The index cards serve as a guide to refer us to our main or major information source. We have reduced the population from several hundred to a manageable number of five or six.

Another manual method is to have lists typed up in alphabetical order (See Figure 5.3). These lists serve, again, as our guide. We can review the lists and reduce the number of candidates to a manageable number. At this point, having identified individuals who possess the required background, we can go to their personnel folders or to some other more extensive information source. If the group is small enough, we may want to start individual interviews at the same time as we review the personnel folders.

There are other types of manual and manual/machine systems making use of various retrieval techniques. In each case, the aim is the same—to reduce the population to a manageable number, so that a more detailed study and/or interview of the people can be performed. Should your situation be one where a manual system is feasible, always keep this goal in mind when making a decision on the system to be used.

COMPUTER

The decision as to when to use a computer for processing a skills inventory can be difficult. There is never a clear-cut number of employees that dictates going from a manual system to an automated or computer system. As was mentioned earlier, the complexity

MANUAL INDEX CARDS
SKILLS INVENTORY

Name _____

Employee No. _____

(Key Word)
_____

Date _____

Figure 5-1

Name _____

Employee No. _____

(Work Experience)
_____

Date _____

Figure 5-2

MANUAL LISTS
SKILLS INVENTORIES

Example of language lists:

Language	Proficiency	Employee Number	Employee Name
French	Fluent	01245	R. L. Jones
French	Fluent	32146	R. S. Smith
French	Read and write	41785	B. L. Brown
French	Read	21643	A. G. Green
German	Fluent	31624	J. B. Jones
German	Read	16348	R. L. Black
German	Read	81946	S. J. White
Spanish	Fluent	20153	D. J. Green
Spanish	Read and write	89321	C. T. Brown
Spanish	Read and write	46857	R. J. Blue
Spanish	Read	12485	B. W. Name
Spanish	Read	52167	R. T. Bronson

Figure 5-3

and variety of the skills being performed may be more of a deciding factor in the degree of automation than the actual numbers of people.

The question of using or not using a computerized or automated system must be balanced against the manual or other options. As with any other systems decision, the economic or financial consideration is usually the deciding factor. Basically, there is a point at which both time and money are saved by further automation.

This is an area that needs to be continually reviewed. As technology advances, changes tend to make automation a more viable option. Even if the costs of an automated system are too high at one point in time, the feasibility of automation should be reconsidered at regular intervals. In fact, a new advancement may bring costs to a point where automation becomes a sound investment within a short period of time.

Assuming that the data is already stored on a computer, or that we have decided to go with such a system based on a cost study, there are many ways of setting up the computer interface with the skills system.

Remember, the automated portion of the system is normally used for storage and processing. We want to take advantage of the enhanced speed and retrieval capability. The way in which this is approached can have a direct impact on our costs and the benefits, or lack of them, in using automation.

We have multiple options and combinations in using a computer system. The skills inventory can be the gold-plated variety with all the "bells and whistles," or a very plain system interfacing with the computer for only part of the job to be done. There are situations where going first class is justified, and there are situations where going coach is appropriate. Each firm or organization must make its own decisions based on its unique inventory needs and requirements.

Let us take a brief look at a few of the options that we have in selecting a computer system. First, if at present we have a computer within the firm it has certain capabilities and limitations. On the other hand, we are not limited (unless by internal policy) to this specific computer system. There is an ever-increasing availability of outside computer services that can be rented or leased. Some are units that are delivered, while others offer connections via telephone lines to a main computer system perhaps thousands of miles away. In today's world there is no lack of technical options in setting up an inventory system. On the contrary, the problem may be the large number of choices that must be studied and analyzed.

Some of the more advanced systems tie directly into the computer via a terminal. This terminal may be typewriter in style, where the inquiries are typed in and responses are printed back. It may be a video screen, where the inquiries and responses are shown on a television type monitor. These are often supported by a printer so that if necessary a hard copy of the response can be obtained.

The terminal access has a number of advantages, assuming the supporting computer programs have been written accordingly. This type of operation can be set up to allow inquiry of the computer, or at least the inventory files as the need arises. For example, a search request is received for a CPA who speaks fluent Spanish. Under a terminal access system that has been properly programmed, we can go to the terminal, make the inquiry and receive the printed listing back. Depending on the program and system parameters, the waiting time is greatly minimized. This can be important in making a management decision. There is a very real value, though most difficult to quantify, in being able to ask a question and get the answer or data back almost immediately. There is a very real cost involved in having the convenience of rapid turnaround or response time.

Many systems make use of computers without the direct computer inquiry. The searches are "batch processed" through the computer. Here the search requests are run together at one time, rather than individually as they occur. This may be significantly less expensive, since it is more efficient, and computer time can be adequately scheduled.

Each computer system has its capabilities and limitations. In addition, each organization has policy procedures for access to and use of this system. Often the existing computer system may be able to fully support the requirements of the skills inventory. However, the use of the computer system for the skills inventory processing and search may be limited due to the internal policies and procedures of the organization. It is up to those involved to explore the alternatives. Something can be technically possible, but politically impossible, and it is important to be aware of the difference.

ALTERNATIVES AND VARIATIONS

There are many systems operating that use automated techniques, but are not necessarily computer systems in the truest sense of the word. We often see systems where the data has been transferred to punched cards and sorted and listed directly from the cards. This method can be time-consuming to operate, but still be effective to use. However, as the price of computer access has gone down, this method is often hard to cost justify.

Microfilm has been used to record and store skills inventory data for a long time. This will be discussed in more detail in a later chapter, but it is significant to note here. There have been major advances in microfilm, not only in the processing and quality of microfilm, but in the retrieval systems that are available. It is the latter that has been of major interest to those using skills inventories. Microfilm systems are now available that can sort and retrieve data in volume. This makes these systems viable contenders for use in inventories.

6

INVENTORY OUTPUT FORMS

OUTPUT POSSIBILITIES

The type of data base established will determine the options we have in getting information back out of the system. A computer-based data file will probably give us the greatest number of options and the most flexibility. Programs can be established to display the data in the various combinations that might be of use. Here we have one of the most important decisions. What do we need or want to use?

The data captured may be highly accurate and the processing may be highly sophisticated, but that is only part of the function. The reason we set up skills inventories is to be able to search for the data and get selected information. In setting up the output system we have to analyze and project our future requirements. We need to find out ahead of time what questions will be asked of the system and to provide a format for this response. Many systems are excellent in data capture and processing, but neglect this aspect. These systems often either fail, or they fall into disuse.

There are several ways of determining the types of questions and thus the output format that will be required. One is to survey the industry and see what others are using. It is tragic, but many people overlook this option and try to re-invent the wheel. They may well be too embarrassed, internally too secretive, or whatever the case may be, to take the time to find out what other related organizations are doing in this area. This is a shame, since even close competitors are usually willing to share their ideas on skills inventories.

Remember, a skills inventory is not usually a trade secret. There is no magical or mystical innovation involved that is going to be worth hiding. By the very nature of the system, secrecy is almost impossible. Employees are involved from the very beginning. We have had them supply data and very probably reviewed it with them. Also, there is normally heavy advertising in the local house organ or other media to announce the new system or keep an active system ongoing. This is one way of gaining acceptance and overcoming resistance to change. Most firms try to achieve a fair measure of employee interest, involvement and support of their skills inventories. It is only in this way that we can ensure a steady flow of accurate and updated information.

As can be seen, there is usually little reluctance to share general information about the system. We are not asking for specific information, names or numbers; just samples of the types of output forms the system uses. Most firms will supply sample packages on request and this can be a good way to review alternate possibilities.

SELECTING SAMPLE FIRMS

When seeking to review the skills inventories of other organizations there are several things to keep in mind. First, it is going to be more useful if the data is compatible with our activity. In essence, medium-sized canning firms would want to review those in the same or related industries. If this information is not available at least try to obtain material from organizations of the same size in regards to the number of people employed and the level of skills involved. Commonality and compatibility of information is more apt to be found in this type of situation.

Another important factor is the success of the inventory system we are reviewing. If we are looking at another organization's output forms for possible future use, we need to ascertain how effective this system has been. Are they satisfied with the results being achieved? What is the level of employee participation? What type of feedback do they get from line managers? We want to be certain we are patterning what we are doing on a success model and not on one that is failing. If a system is not adequate, see if you can find out why. The chances are good that you may learn what the problems have been and what possible future corrective action can be taken. It is by focusing on this corrective action that we can gain some insight which will help us avoid a future costly error of our own.

There are packages that have already been developed and are marketed. These can also provide leads. In fact, you might locate one that ideally meets your requirements. Again, try to find one that comes close to your organization's requirements as far as type of product and size of operation is concerned. Even if a purchase is not made, the salesperson representing the package can be helpful. Usually, he/she will have experience with many organizations going through exactly what you are experiencing. Do not hesitate to ask for a list of previous clients and specific referrals. These are good sources, not only to verify the background of the salesperson, but to give you a possible list of experienced managers with whom to discuss your endeavor. They can suggest shortcuts and new ideas you may not have considered.

BASIC OUTPUT FORMATS

Most organizations produce a biography type of document on each employee from the skills inventory system. This is usually a modified résumé (See Figure 6.1). It shows the employee's name, department, identification number, and other pertinent information at the top. This is generally referred to as "home room" information. Then the factual skills inventory data such as key words, work experience, education, language proficiency, special courses, professional memberships, vocational licenses, position and location preferences. Included here would be any important items the firm chooses to have as part of their inventory, such as hobbies, social clubs, publications, etc.

This biographical sketch or employee biography serves a dual purpose. It gives the employee a complete reading of his/her status as it exists on the skills inventory system. Secondly, it gives management a reference point. It closely resembles a résumé and is used for the same purpose. The manager can review in more depth candidates basically meeting his/her qualifications.

For example, say twenty candidates meet the basic requirements

BIOGRAPHY

Name: __xx x x x x x x__   Date Prepared: __xx-xx-xx__
Department: __x x x x__   Mail Code: __xxx__
Social Security No.: __xx-xx-xxxx__

Key Words: *Work Experience:*

                                  From   *To*   *Type*

	From	To	Type
x x x x x x x x x x x	xx-xx	xx-xx	x x x x x x x x x x x
x x x x x x x x x x x	xx-xx	xx-xx	x x x x x x x x x x x
x x x x x x x x x x x	xx-xx	xx-xx	x x x x x x x x x x x

Education: *Language:*

Degree	Major	College	Name	Proficiency
xx	x x x x x x	x x x x x x	x x x x x x	x x
xx	x x x x x x	x x x x x x	x x x x x x	x x

Special Courses: *Professional Memberships:*

Date	Name	Date	Name
xx-xx	x x x x x x x x x	xx-xx	x x x x x x x x x x x
xx-xx	x x x x x x x x x	xx-xx	x x x x x x x x x x x

Vocational   *Position*   *Location*
Licenses: *Preference:*   *Preference:*

    x x x x x x x x x   x x x x x x x x x   x x x x x x x x x

    x x x x x x x x x   x x x x x x x x x   x x x x x x x x x

Figure 6-1

specified for a given position. Most managers would not want to go through personnel folder reviews on this many people, let alone interview them at this stage. Here is where the biography is valuable. It is normally only a one- or two-page document showing the various skill areas, which helps make it easy to reduce the candidate list to a manageable number. In the same manner as screening résumés, the most qualified people are identified for further review. The twenty biographies can be reduced to five or eight that show the best overall background. A personnel folder review at this stage can further reduce the number involved. Ultimately, we have reduced the group to be interviewed to a manageable number. This is a very valuable tool for a busy manager.

Another basic output format for a skills inventory system would be the capability to produce computer or machine run listings. These listings are more effective when we can identify and change the information which goes into them. We just finished discussing doing a search and identifying twenty names that met certain parameters. At this point we would select the corresponding biography. If a capability to search and print a listing of the twenty names was available, then the biographies would not have to be created each time. They could all be run at one time, then stored in an external file in order of employee number, alphabetical, social security numbers, or whatever method was selected. A listing could be produced showing only possible names and social security numbers (See Figure 6.2). This concept allows us to use the computer or machine maintained file as an index.

Another method that uses a combination of listings and biographies adds one additional feature. The biographies are also printed and stored external to the computer system. In addition, an index, or set of indexes, is also printed and maintained in a binder external to the computer. These indexes are the most commonly searched terms (skills inventory categories) sorted in alphabetical order. Within the alphabetical order is a cross-reference to the employee's social security number (employee number) and/or employee names (See Figure 6.3).

This system provides certain savings in computer time and printing. Also, there is no dependence on the computer being available to

CANDIDATE LIST

Name	Social Security No.
1. Jones, R. L.	XOO-XX-OOOO
2. Smith, S. V.	XOX-OO-XXXX
3. Brown, R. Z.	XXX-XO-XXXX
4. Green, L.	XXO-OO-OOXX
5. Black, T. J.	XOO-XO-XXOO
6. Fredrick, R. T.	XXO-XX-XOOX
20. Thomas, G. L.	XXO-OX-XOOO

Figure 6-2

LANGUAGE INDEX

Language	Proficiency	Employee Name	Social Security No.
Dutch	Fluent	x x x x x x x , x x	xxx-xx-xxxx
Dutch	Fluent	x x x x x x x , x x	xxx-xx-xxxx
Dutch	Read	x x x x x x x , x x	xxx-xx-xxxx
Dutch	Write	x x x x x x x , x x	xxx-xx-xxxx
French	Fluent	x x x x x x x , x x	xxx-xx-xxxx
French	Fluent	x x x x x x x , x x	xxx-xx-xxxx
French	Fluent	x x x x x x x , x x	xxx-xx-xxxx
French	Read	x x x x x x x , x x	xxx-xx-xxxx
French	Write	x x x x x x x , x x	xxx-xx-xxxx
French	Write	x x x x x x x , x x	xxx-xx-xxxx
German	Fluent	x x x x x x x , x x	xxx-xx-xxxx
German	Fluent	x x x x x x x , x x	xxx-xx-xxxx
German	Read	x x x x x x x , x x	xxx-xx-xxxx
German	Read	x x x x x x x , x x	xxx-xx-xxxx
German	Read	x x x x x x x , x x	xxx-xx-xxxx

Note: Sorted alphabetically by language then by proficiency.

Figure 6-3

conduct a search. The computer is used annually, semi-annually or quarterly to produce new biographies and indexes. The time frames on this will depend on the amount of activity within the organization. If there is high turnover, large numbers of new hires, major transfer activity, etc.—a more rapid or frequent update may be desirable. In the event the organization is stable, an annual run of these products may be more than sufficient.

In any case, the search activity can be conducted rapidly in the external environment without the dependence on the computer being available when a search request is received. This really provides very rapid turnaround to those requesting a search. Depending on the nature of the organization this may be a significant factor. In some cases it may be critical to perform internal searches very rapidly. One example would be where a customer has arrived who speaks a foreign language and a translator is needed. Waiting for a computer listing could cause serious problems, since in this case time is of the essence.

Providing computer or machine run listings as output has other uses and implications. Assuming the skills inventory data is loaded into an automated file retrieval system, there are significant statistical uses. Often the information can be combined with payroll data such as salary rate, performance rating, etc., to give additional information in decision making (See Figure 6.4). This can be a very valuable tool for management.

One area that needs to be explored in depth, if the inventory is to be used for purely statistical purposes, is the participation rate. Payroll data, by its very nature, accounts for all employees. They must be included to receive a pay check. Skills inventory data does not necessarily have the same degree of participant motivation. In fact, some skills inventory data banks rely on voluntary submission for the information.

There is often a sound basis for this lack of complete skills inventory data. These systems are usually developed or tacked onto the existing files which an organization maintains. In most cases skills inventories are recent developments and are looked on as additional or supplemental data sources. This concept seems to be

STATISTICAL LISTING

Note: This listing is used to determine the average rate and performance ratings of people with tax accounting background (or showing this as a key word).

Key Word	Salary Rate	Performance Rating
Tax accounting	$ 15,000	8
Tax accounting	20,000	8
Tax accounting	20,000	10
Tax accounting	25,000	10
Tax accounting	15,000	7
Tax accounting	20,000	10
Tax accounting	25,000	9
Tax accounting	20,000	8
Tax accounting	15,000	10
Tax accounting	25,000	8
Total 10	$200,000	88
Average	$ 20,000	8.8

Figure 6-4

changing as more and more people become aware of the strengths and value of maintaining a strong and current system.

The statistical requirements of most organizations can be satisfied to a greater degree by a complete and updated inventory system. There is a large volume of information captured on a skills inventory that would be valuable for many internal studies and reports. As management is becoming aware of this important statistical impact, more effort is being made to insure file completion.

There are other solutions to achieving greater employee participation. Many of these will be discussed in detail later in this section. However, from a technical point of view we usually have a very effective way to ensure data is captured. This system is usually referred to as the main payroll system. In any organization that has a sufficient number of employees to warrant considering a skills inventory, the payroll is processed in a relatively sophisticated manner or in an automated manner.

At the same time, there are fairly strict controls over the payroll processing as far as the data and follow-up on incomplete data are concerned. Forms or procedures are established to get people into the system, complete the required individual income tax information, etc. Paychecks do not go out without fairly strict control over current information such as pay rate, shift, hours worked, etc. In most cases the operation is given frequent internal audits to ensure all information is properly accounted for.

This systems concept seems to have the type of follow-up necessary to ensure an up-to-date skills inventory system for statistical purposes. There are also possibilities for insuring, at least mechanical accuracy in processing information, to give us a highly reliable output. It is this type of accuracy and reliability that is desired as a base to prepare statistical reports of similar quality.

Ideally, tying the skills inventory into the checks and balances of this system is worthy of consideration. It is not always practical or feasible to do this. There are both operating considerations and varying political considerations in all organizations that must be taken into account. It is suggested that this area be given a thorough review for consideration as a vehicle to enhance the accuracy of the skills inventory system.

TURNAROUND DOCUMENT

The turnaround document that was discussed as an input document is also a very effective output document (See Figure 6.5). This document is extremely useful in an automated system, since the actual, or most currently stored information can be printed directly on the form and returned to the employee. This allows us to complete a full cycle of input, processing and output (See Figure 6.6). This is in contrast to the standard form.

One of the various positive points of this document is that we do not have the employee continually being forced to search for the form to be filled out. When using a standard form the employee sometimes cannot find the form or, when the form is found, it is an obsolete copy. Nothing is more frustrating that to submit a form and have it returned with a note "Obsolete—use June Revision" or words to that effect. This seems to occur even when specific instructions were sent out detailing the destruction of an obsolete form before the new version is released.

The turnaround document is not totally immune to obsolesence, since people are often asked to retain them until a change is warranted. This can also create the problem of how to handle one that gets lost. Normally, some procedure must be provided to handle the lost or missing turnaround. It has to be reprinted or, if the current information is known, provision for a change on a blank document has to be available.

UPDATING THE DOCUMENT

One method of resolving obsolete file copies and partially handling lost documents is having the employees periodically update their information. Forms for all employees have to be updated depending on a schedule related to the organization's nature and the type of staff. A frequent update, say quarterly or semi-annually, is usually sufficient to handle the obsolete forms retained in the file. It must be remembered that most employees do not change their background, and few people add a new degree or any other major skills category

Planning and Using Skills Inventory Systems

TURNAROUND DOCUMENT

<u>Sample</u>

NAME: R. L. Jones

DEPARTMENT: 68-00

SOCIAL SECURITY NUMBER: XXX-XX-XXXX

EDUCATION:

	Degree	Major	College
<u>Actual</u>			
1	B.S.	Bus. Admin.	U.C.L.A.
2			
<u>Correction/Change</u>			
1			
2			

LANGUAGES:

	Name	Proficiency
<u>Actual</u>		
1	French	Read
2	Spanish	Read and write
3		
<u>Correction/Change</u>		
1		
2		
3		

Figure 6-5

Inventory Output Forms 77

TURNAROUND FORM VERSUS STANDARD FORM

TURNAROUND CYCLE

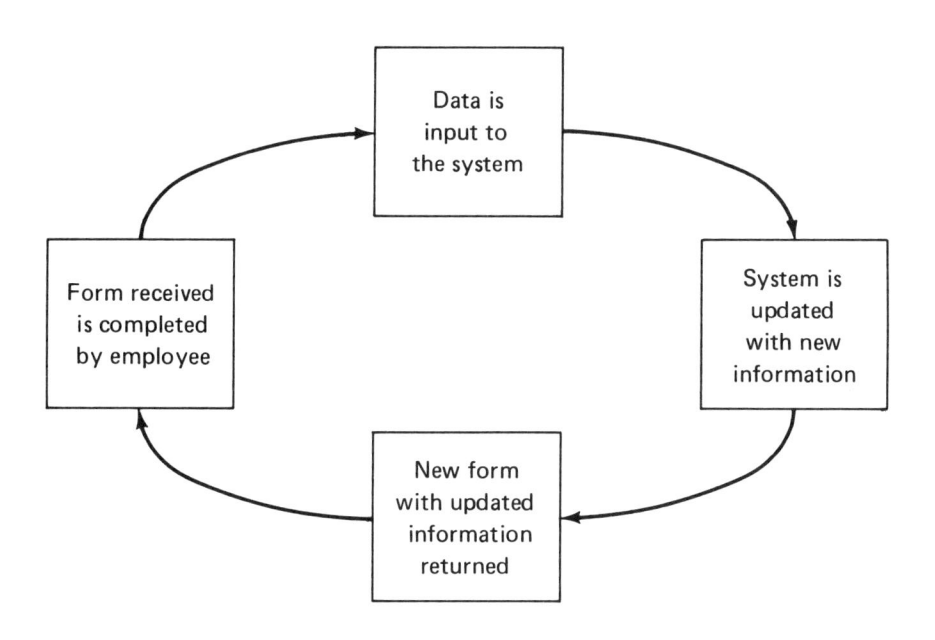

Form received is completed by employee → Data is input to the system → System is updated with new information → New form with updated information returned → (back to Form received is completed by employee)

STANDARD FORM

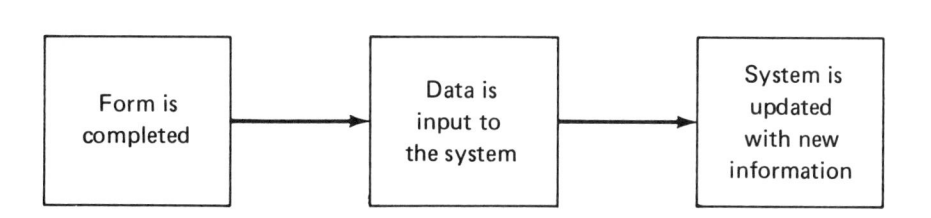

Form is completed → Data is input to the system → System is updated with new information

Figure 6-6

that often. It is generally sufficient to send out an update to all employees on an annual basis.

Some organizations also have voluntary updates on a monthly basis. This is for those employees who are new to the system, making a voluntary change, or for those who have lost the form. This update just handles the changes and is not sent out to everyone, but only to the small percentage that have activity during the current month.

In an automated system this keeps the cost of running single changes down, since they are grouped and sent through on a monthly basis. This type of turnaround seems satisfactory for the employees, since acquiring new skills takes a long time and patience. When compared to the months or years of schooling or training involved in getting the new skill, a few weeks wait to see it reflected seems a relatively short period or time. Management also seems to be able to live with this type of time frame. When searching the file, the chances of missing someone who has submitted an update is small. Normally, less than five percent would ever be voluntarily updating during any month.

In this situation it must be noted that many employees will probably not voluntarily update. Many will wait until all biographies are sent out on the "forced" update which occurs in most organizations on an annual basis. Still, the percentage amount of skills acquired in one year is probably not high enough to have an impact on search. The previously discussed problem of some employees not submitting any data—the participation rate—is the item of greatest concern with most inventories.

PSYCHOLOGICAL REINFORCEMENT

Another important value of a turnaround document is partly psychological in nature. This is that all involved become familiar with the form and with the system as a whole. Often we send something back and wonder about whether the recipient got it, and if so whether anything was done about it. The standard form falls into this category. The output is not always there to provide any reinforcement for the action taken.

We discussed an annual update where all biographies, whether blank or not, are sent to employees. This can also have an impact on an individual and be an added incentive to completing and submitting a biography. Most people don't want to think of themselves as being a "blank." If this type of annual update is coupled with a monthly voluntary update, the information can be returned to the submitting employee quite rapidly. Most firms can gear up once a year to respond to a large group of biographies. The monthly update may seem slower, but not all employees submit their changes or corrections exactly at the beginning of the month, or at the end. Consequently, the waiting time might be only a few weeks.

DESIGN OF DOCUMENT

Special care must be taken to ensure the form is given special design consideration. First, most forms are going to be printed on a medium or high speed printer. Alignment must be properly established to allow for this. Secondly, the form must allow space for employee input.

Most firms either have an in-house consultant or can hire one—many forms manufacturers provide such a service—to ensure the machine design is adequate. The greatest problem may be to deal with designing the form adequately for employee input. Here the items have to allow sufficient space for writing, since most people have varying styles. Of even greater importance is the coordination of the form with the instruction manual.

This is particularly true where the forms are being filled out by the employee with little or no outside assistance. In most cases we will have someone proof the form prior to entry into the system. However, if the form and examples are properly coordinated, this task will be made much easier. By the same token, there is less chance of an error getting through to a computerized system.

Properly prepared forms that have been closely coordinated with the instructions can save significant time and money. As indicated earlier it is very wise to "pilot test" the forms and instructions before putting them into wide use. It is a good idea to use several pilot groups made up of all levels of experience and education that might be asked to participate in the final system. It is much less embarrassing, much easier and also less costly to make the changes before sending out several hundred or a thousand.

The question always arises as to how many copies of the inventory form or biography should be produced. As with any other system this may vary according to the organization structure and policy. It would be fairly safe to state that three or four copies are close to the standard number in circulation for most skills inventories. Possible distribution would include a copy for a skills inventory center, one for the main personnel file, one for the supervisor, and one for the employee. Some alternate distribution patterns are shown in Figure 6.7 and Figure 6.8.

In Figure 6.8 the supervisor was left out of immediate distribution. Most firms have a central personnel file. Here management has access to information on employees. This level of information is sometime restricted in nature (e.g., first line supervision may have limited access). Skills inventory data is also personal in nature showing information such as education, years of experience, etc. It is often policy to restrict distribution of this information, and to set limits as to the level of management that has access to it. Much the same limitations are applied as to any other personnel file document.

The two figures show some common distribution patterns. These certainly are not all inclusive. Document distribution patterns can vary significantly between divisions or departments within the same organization. Some may have eight or more copies floating around. If this be the case, certainly any confidentiality is most probably lost.

The quality of printing usually diminishes with the number of copies made. This, of course, depends on the equipment used, impact paper, carbon paper, etc. used to print additional copies. In the past a four-part carbon paper form was a reasonable limit. Even here, if the printer had not been properly maintained, the fourth copy was fuzzy and hard to read. Often supervisors or the organization keeps the better file copies and passes those of less quality on down the line. In this case we should be certain the employee gets a good copy. Remember, with the turnaround document the employee is the key to the future changes and corrections.

DISTRIBUTION PATTERNS
SKILLS INVENTORY FORMS

ALTERNATE 1
Four Copies

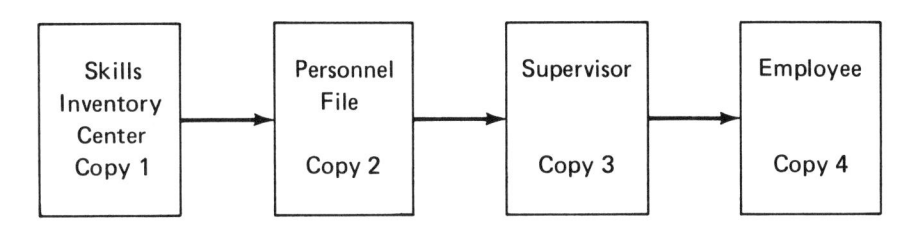

Skills Inventory Center Copy 1 → Personnel File Copy 2 → Supervisor Copy 3 → Employee Copy 4

Figure 6-7

ALTERNATE 2
Three Copies

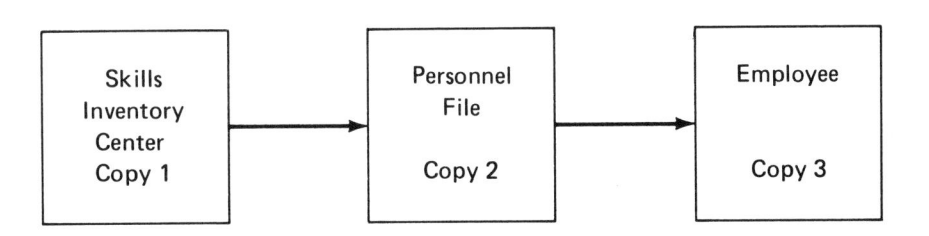

Skills Inventory Center Copy 1 → Personnel File Copy 2 → Employee Copy 3

Figure 6-8

82 Planning and Using Skills Inventory Systems

The number of pages for a biography is another consideration. A turnaround document requires additional space since it must display the output, plus make room for the employee to make changes or corrections. Ideally, we would like to get everything on one page. However, if the information required is extensive, this may not be possible. In the long run, two or more pages with sufficient writing room for the employee may be more advisable.

7
INTERNAL DESIGN CONSIDERATIONS

ORGANIZATIONAL TERMS

Organizations tend to develop a personality of their own. They are bound together by a common objective or product line. Sometimes the requirement for secrecy keeps them from having a great deal of outside contact. The reasons for this secrecy may range all the way from national security to a simple desire to protect a competitive position. After a while this seems to develop into a club or "old school" type of atmosphere.

Even those organizations that are open, and free from any type of internal secrecy, still tend to develop a unique personality. Those people who have shared common experiences tend to develop a common bond. This an interesting sidelight on human nature. Organizations develop these personality traits because they are made up of human beings. Human beings have distinct and predictable group behavior patterns which are manifested in the personality of the organization itself.

One of the characteristics that evolves is a unique organizational language. In some cases this reaches a significant level of development and use. At times, a person almost feels a need to go to language school just to communicate with his/her new organization. It is as if you were trying to communicate with a foreign country.

This is a very real feeling and may indeed be a similar in nature to dealing with a foreign country. The organization, to some degree, can be an isolated group. It depends on its own members for its strength and their contributions cause it to grow and prosper. By the same token, lack of contribution can have the opposite effect. Everyone is somewhat apprehensive about the unknown and organizations are certainly no different, since they also are made up of people.

Just as language can be the key to communication between countries, it can also be the key to communication for an organization. Have you ever noted the somewhat strained communication which occurs between a person in the military and a civilian? Both can be from the same state and city, but communications problems can and do arise. There is a distinct difference in the language developed in the military organization.

These organizational language patterns are very significant. A good example of these is to be found in the diplomatic corps, where the use or lack of use of a simple phrase or word can have tremendous impact on the interpretation of an entire communication. The significance of this is so great that most of us cannot even begin to understand a diplomatic message without the benefit of an experienced interpreter.

Within an organization there are additional pockets of language use, almost like mini foreign states within a country. If the organization has a union or bargaining unit, there will be many different contracts. Here we have the language of employee relations or labor relations, which is truly a unique body of words and phrases. Each of these used in or out of context can impart a changed, new or opposing meaning.

In another area of an organization there often exists a legal group or department, and at least part of the reason for their existence is for the interpretation of words and phrases. We often forget the complexity involved here until we have to read a contract before purchasing a house or car, or when we review our own wills. In those circumstances most of us have a helpless feeling and know that we have to depend blindly on an expert's analysis and interpretation.

WORDS AND INVENTORIES

The entire skills inventory system is made up of a body of words. It is through the proper combination and use of words that we have an accurate and functionally effective system, and these words are obviously critical to an inventory. It is for this reason that so much time and consideration needs to be spent in their development.

Too often this area becomes overlooked in the system development. It is very easy to find other areas of concern and focus attention on them. The selection of the hardware that will be used for processing, or the design of the folder and accompanying instructions can draw us off track like a siren's song. These areas are much more interesting and exciting to work with—the processing package alone can involve significant dollar outlay. There are vendors to deal with, budget discussions, implementation meetings, etc. All of these seem to have more to offer, or appear to be of greater significance or meaning, than working with the design of the words and the corresponding word system that will be used.

Structuring the word package is pick and shovel work. Yet, it is very important pick and shovel work. It is one part of the system that we are going to have to live with for a long time to come. Most of the other parts of the package can be changed with a lot less overall disruption. The processing package can be changed and probably will be over the life of the system. It is not uncommon to go from a manual system to an automated one, or from one form of computer to a new generation. The folder and accompanying instructions will also be changed and modified as new needs occur.

The words or language used in the system will probably remain fairly constant. There will be some additions and deletions to the key words, professional organizations, foreign languages, etc., but not major revisions. Should major revisions occur it will be nearly the same as throwing out the existing skills inventory and starting over. It is the word system that dictates the nature and scope of the entire skills inventory. To change this is to change the largest segment of the system.

THE ORGANIZATION'S LANGUAGE

We have said each organization has a language. This language is made up of words and phrases. We have also said that it is these that make up the skills inventory system. Because we have placed these words at the pinnacle of importance, we need to discuss some of the ways of achieving an accurate and representative word system to begin with, one that is both useful, and one that is flexible for present and for future requirements. It should be designed so that when it is accepted and locked into place, we can rely on its continuing usefulness in years to come.

One approach is to take an existing skills inventory word system and use it as a starting point. Remember, we are talking about a starting point only, and not plugging it in totally. There is a very great difference. Later we will be talking in more detail about package systems that are sold by vendors. It should be pointed out here that one of the considerations in purchasing a system is the flexibility of the word package offered. Do they want to have you use the system without any modification? If so, is the existing system being used satisfactorily by an organization or preferably, several organizations, identical to yours?

These are very important concerns and considerations. Ideally, we want the word package or system to be tailored to our organization. This is something that we want to control fully, regardless of whether the system is designed internally or purchased from a vendor.

Whichever choice is made, there are some important steps that should be taken. The first is to get sample packages that are used by similar organizations. For example, you can select one currently in use by a related engineering firm, should this be your area of work. If you are using a vendor they will probably have several options to show you that they have used on organizations similar to yours.

Next and possibly the most important step, is to verify the information in the word package. The word "verify" is used here in the sense that the word package must be shown to stand up under actual scrutiny within the organization.

One of the best ways of doing this is to utilize the resources within the organization. There are many years of experience in the management of the firm. Most department managers are more than qualified to review the word packages for their areas.

To complete the review may take several passes (See Figure 7.1). As indicated earlier there may be a requirement after the first cut to

Internal Design Considerations 87

REVIEW OF WORD SYSTEMS
(TERMS AND KEY WORDS)

```
┌─────────────────────────────┐
│         Initial             │
│       word system           │
│   (Terms and key words)     │
└─────────────────────────────┘
              │
              ▼
┌─────────────────────────────┐
│          Review             │
│            by               │
│        management           │
└─────────────────────────────┘
              │
              ▼
┌─────────────────────────────┐
│          Group              │
│         meetings            │
└─────────────────────────────┘
              │
              ▼
┌─────────────────────────────┐
│         Revised             │
│       word system           │
│   (Terms and key words)     │
└─────────────────────────────┘
              │
              ▼
┌─────────────────────────────┐
│        Additional           │
│        review by            │
│        management           │
└─────────────────────────────┘
              │
              ▼
┌─────────────────────────────┐
│         Finalized           │
│       word system           │
│   (Terms and key words)     │
└─────────────────────────────┘
```

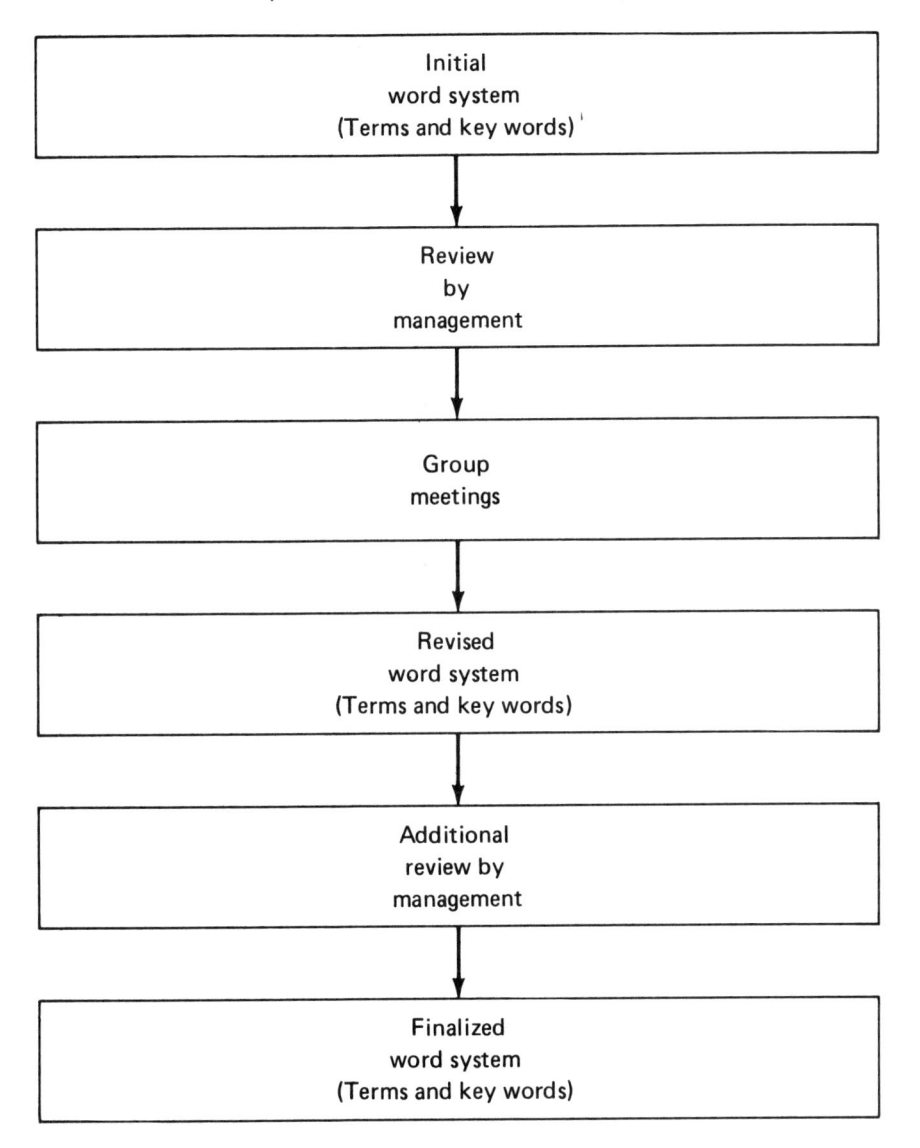

Figure 7-1

hold some group meetings to resolve differences. There will be instances where one manager wants to delete a section and another wants to add to it or expand it. This is both healthy and to be expected. When the problems are resolved you will have a good understanding of the system and the word groups.

If the words are reviewed, edited and approved by the organization's management, the terms are going to be consistent with those used in the organization. Special or unique words will automatically be included. Those words that are foreign, obsolete, or otherwise meaningless to the organization will be excluded. This approach has allowed us to establish a set of realistic and accurate terms and key words.

REQUISITION SYSTEM

All organizations possess a requisition system of one form or another. This is the way a manager or supervisor goes about requesting and getting approval for a new employee. This may be as a replacement for someone who has left the group or as an addition to staff caused from an increase in workload or the emergence of a new function or functions.

The inventory has more credibility if it is directly tied to the requisition system (See Figure 7.2). This means that all requisitions are tested against the skills inventory system before any selection is made. The concept applies both to transfer activity as well as to going outside the organization and hiring people off the street.

Assume a supervisor has an opening. If the size of the organization is small, the fact that there is an opening may be known by everyone. In larger organizations it may be known by a relatively small percentage of people depending on how the formal and informal lines of communication work and function.

In certain smaller organizations it is possible that everyone is aware of the opening. Certain supervisors may recommend employees they feel are qualified. Employees may approach the supervisor with an opening and ask to be considered. Yet, this still does not mean that everyone who can do the job has been identified. In fact,

Internal Design Considerations 89

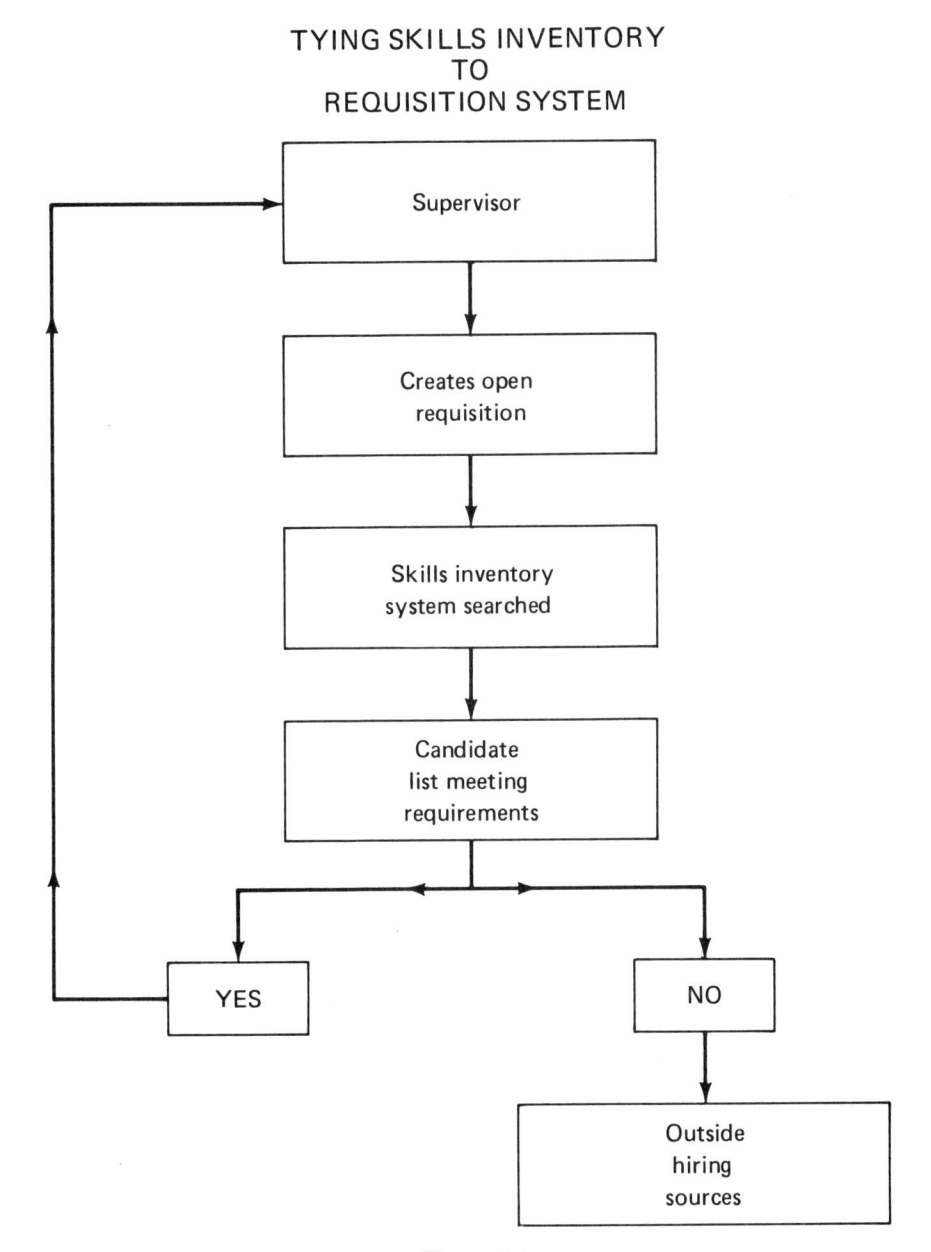

TYING SKILLS INVENTORY TO REQUISITION SYSTEM

```
         Supervisor
             │
             ▼
      Creates open
       requisition
             │
             ▼
     Skills inventory
     system searched
             │
             ▼
       Candidate
      list meeting
      requirements
         ↙     ↘
       YES      NO
        │        │
        │        ▼
        │     Outside
        │      hiring
        │     sources
        └──→ Supervisor
```

Figure 7-2

it does not even begin to ensure that the most qualified have been identified.

How many supervisors are going to volunteer their best staff members to another supervisor who has an opening? Supervisors at the same level usually are in competition with each other. They know their performance depends on having the top people in their area. These people are usually jealously guarded as the valuable asset they actually are to their supervisor. If a supervisor volunteers one of his/her people to another supervisor there may very well be other motives. The employee may be in trouble with his/her present work group, planning to terminate in the near future, has a severe personal problem, etc.

Most management and supervisory training classes stress that managers and supervisors should deal with problem employees rather than transfer them. In reality only a few do this. It is human nature to try to get rid of a problem as rapidly as possible. By the same token, if you can give this problem to a competitor—someone who is vying for the same position you hope to hold in the future—you are even farther ahead. Beware of supervisors "bearing gifts"!

The employee voluntarily seeking a new position stands a better chance of being qualified. There is still the question of why he/she is leaving or wants to leave his/her present position. People often tend to overestimate their own potential. Those that are most aggressive are going to be the ones actively seeking new positions. These are going to be the employees who have a high, or possibly an overvalued opinion of their worth. Though this is not always the case, most experienced supervisors are alerted to it.

In the background may be the employee a supervisor does not want to lose. This may also be a person who is modest about his/her abilities, and is really not actively seeking out a new job opening. At the same time, this is the employee who is highly qualified, and would be interested in an opportunity to advance. This is just the person who is lost to the review of management without a skills inventory.

PROMOTION FROM WITHIN

Many organizations publicize the fact that it is their policy to support promotion from within. This policy and concept is something we want to thoroughly explore when considering the tying of the inventory to the requisition system. When we have this, the stage is set to truly allow for promotion from within.

Normally we are moving people from a lower level job into a higher one. Supposedly this higher level job has more value to the firm. Promoting from within has several advantages. The first one that is usually quoted is employee morale. People like to think their organization is constantly reviewing them for upward mobility and salary opportunities.

To an organization, promotion from within has some hard dollar considerations. A person who is already part of the group does not have to go through a lot of orientation. He/she will know the basic policies, procedures, location of facilities, etc. There is not the break-in period which occurs with a totally new employee, plus the time needed for supervision and other employees to assist in this.

There is the other side of the coin. Employees promoted from within have rather parochial experiences. They do not bring with them the fresh new ideas that the organization may want and need. They have the specific orientation that the organization has given to them over the years. New ideas may not be pursued because "things have not been done that way here." This attitude may automatically reject the ideas the organization is so actively seeking.

Promotion from within certainly does not mean that we will not be hiring from outside. It can actually create a domino effect. Assume someone has quit and left the organization. An opening is in existence, a newly created opening. Most supervisors and managers usually do not admit to having excess staff, except in extreme layoff situations. Under most circumstances they will ask to fill any opening which occurs. Also, there are going to be openings that occur when we do not necessarily have qualified people internally. There will be times when we must go outside to get the fresh new ideas mentioned above. Promotion from within is never total.

OVERCOMING SUPERVISORY RELUCTANCE

This subject has been touched on several times in preceding sections. It seems appropriate to confront it head on at this time. Most managers and supervisors like the idea of being able to identify and hire the most qualified people. All you have to do is bring up the subject and all will readily agree.

Just as we all like nice highways and well-kept parks, but hate the taxes that it takes to support them, most managers and supervisors become reluctant, and even hostile, when it is their own top people that are being considered for other jobs.

Policy has to be clearly established early on as to identifying and releasing candidates located in a search. Questions come up, such as who can look at someone's people? Is there a limit on the number of people taken from one supervisor? Who establishes release dates on candidates? Just use your imagination and you can come up with many more questions. Astute managers probably will not directly question the use of the system. They will postpone implementation through raising a lot of indirect questions. It is important that we anticipate these questions and provide understanding and alternative solutions.

One possible solution is to establish a central skills inventory responsibility (See Figure 7.3). Many organizations center this activity in the personnel department, which acts as a central control or clearing house. Here all requests for searches are received, interviews are scheduled, employee inquiries handled, etc. Policy may be that after a search is reviewed, contact with employees must be made through this central control unit. This can aid in ensuring that a particular supervisor's people are not the only ones interviewed. It can be an aid in ensuring that the most qualified people are available to be interviewed and not just the ones who have a cooperative supervisor.

This type of control unit can never overcome the reluctance of supervisors to lose good people, but it can ensure that policy is administered fairly and that all supervisors obtain equal treatment.

Internal Design Considerations 93

CENTRAL
SKILLS INVENTORY
CONTROL

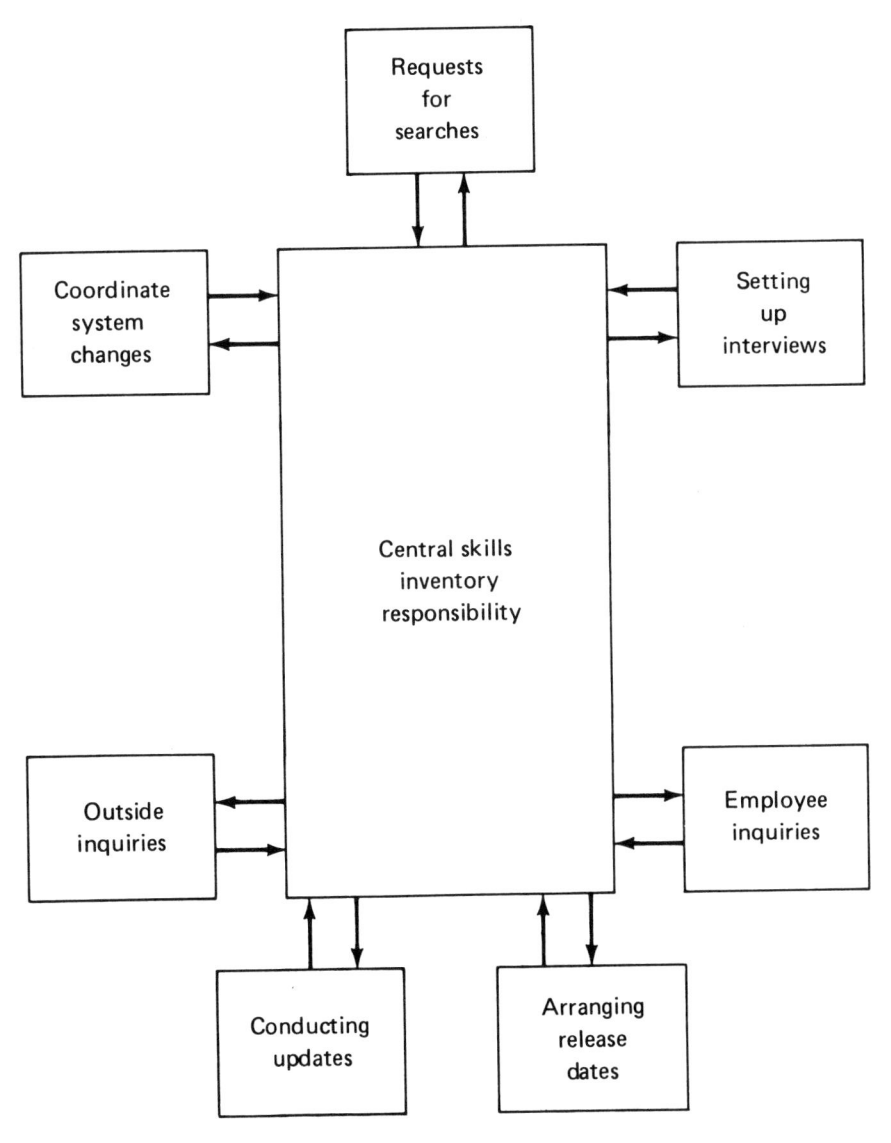

- Requests for searches
- Coordinate system changes
- Setting up interviews
- Central skills inventory responsibility
- Outside inquiries
- Employee inquiries
- Conducting updates
- Arranging release dates

Figure 7-3

If someone loses a top quality person, it can ensure that the replacement is a top quality candidate ready for promotion. This is obviously better than receiving another supervisor's malcontent. There is, or can be, an increase in trust in the system when someone is responsbible for fair and accurate operation.

COMPATIBILITY OF TERMS

As previously noted the terms of selection procedures throughout the organization, should be compatible with the skills inventory. This is particularly true of the requisition system. It is of special importance that the terms used in requesting a replacement in the formal organization process be applicable to the inventory.

If a formal form for requisition is used, we may want to make a modification to it. Assuming we are implementing a skills inventory system, the requisition form is an ideal spot to list selection parameters. At the least we should request that the form include a place to identify the key words, plus any other significant identifiers that would be or should be noted.

This requirement performs several functions. It is a starting point toward bringing management fully on board with the skills inventory. To process a requisition for a replacement they must use the system and identify the appropriate key words. At the same time, the skills inventory is made an integral part of the organization and directly tied to the requisition system.

INVENTORYING OUTSIDE CANDIDATES

The cyclical nature of the employment market has an impact on most organizations. It seems that it is either a feast or a famine. When the unemployment rate is high, there is hesitation to run an advertisement with the firm's name on it. Application letters or résumés will sometimes appear by the hundreds after a blind advertisement is placed—one with just a post office box, but usually no organization name. Making the mistake of naming the organization will deluge one with phone calls and many times the applicants will arrive in person.

This situation can change as rapidly as a flash flood can dry up. Let the unemployment rate go down substantially in an area and applicants and résumés seem to disappear. We turn around and run a large ad with little or no response. Internal recruiting staffs are beefed up. For selected job openings, we go to outside recruiters and pay premium prices for their aid in locating qualified applicants.

Even during stable times, assuming there is such a period, we are usually concerned with filling present openings. It is not uncommon to have a person apply for a job, and for nothing in his/her area to be available at the time of the application. A nice rejection letter is written. Several months later this is the very same area in which three jobs unexpectedly come open.

No one could foresee or project these openings. They were not retirements or training rollovers, they were not of the nature that any manpower planning function could have been expected to anticipate. Even a good "crystal ball" does not function in this type of situation. It is also not uncommon to find that the original résumé or enquiry letter cannot be located. This is particularly true right after an economic downturn when we have been deluged with job seekers.

Sometimes in a large operation, we may not even be aware that anyone with the background currently being sought was even interested. There may be several people interviewing and screening applicants and résumés. The person trying to fill the opening may not have been involved in reviewing or declining the applicants in the prior situation. Even if they were, unless they possess total recall, a certain percentage of these desirable applicants is going to "drop through the crack." The larger the organization, the larger you may assume the "cracks" will be.

INVENTORY APPLICATIONS

The framework for identifying candidates for internal selection by means of skills inventory has been defined and established. What about the use of the systems to identify outside candidates?

It certainly sounds attractive. Being able to retrieve those people previously interviewed, those who were highly qualified, but for whom no present opening existed, could prevent the applicant from being lost when we can no longer find the original résumé. Further, it can allow us to rapidly locate all the individuals who have previously applied who now meet our parameters.

MECHANICS OF AN OUTSIDE CANDIDATE SYSTEM

There are several approaches to setting up an outside candidate system. File size may dictate that we keep our outside system separate from the internal system. Search costs may be too high if we co-mingle the external and internal files. Doing this will depend on such factors as the type of computer or other system used, anticipated number of people on the system, storage capacity, etc.

It actually is not hard to keep the internal separated from the external. A simple code indicating an active employee versus an applicant will serve this purpose. Most of the constraints deal with the hardware problems involved. Consultation with a data processing expert in the organization can quickly resolve this question. Frequently, the decision will be made to go with separate files—one being dedicated to internal use and one to external. The important thing here is that the decision is compatible with the internal system and policies.

Capturing of the data to set up the system should follow a normal course (See Figure 7.4). Candidates that are identified for possible future need can be so informed. Then they may be provided with an inventory form to complete, or the interviewer can fill one out for them. Ideally, it would save time if the form were completed by the applicant. The form would be reviewed for accuracy and completeness, and then forwarded for entry into the system.

Some people hesitate to request applicants to complete an inventory form. It is standard practice to provide a qualified candidate with an application form, so why not a skills inventory form? Most organizations send out a letter to the effect that, "We regret to inform ... your application will be kept in our active file, should an opening occur we will be in touch with you." No one, especially an outside applicant, ever expects anything to come of this.

Providing someone with a skills inventory form indicates the

EXTERNAL APPLICANT DATA CAPTURE

```
┌─────────────────────────────────┐
│        Review of                │
│        potential                │
│        applicants               │
└─────────────────────────────────┘
                │
                ▼
┌─────────────────────────────────┐
│       Identify those            │
│   qualified for possible        │
│       future openings           │
└─────────────────────────────────┘
                │
                ▼
┌─────────────────────────────────┐
│          Notify                 │
│         applicant               │
│      of his/her status          │
└─────────────────────────────────┘
                │
                ▼
┌─────────────────────────────────┐
│          Request                │
│       completion of             │
│       inventory forms           │
└─────────────────────────────────┘
                │
                ▼
┌─────────────────────────────────┐
│      Review completed           │
│          form for               │
│          accuracy               │
└─────────────────────────────────┘
                │
                ▼
┌─────────────────────────────────┐
│         Enter into              │
│          system                 │
└─────────────────────────────────┘
```

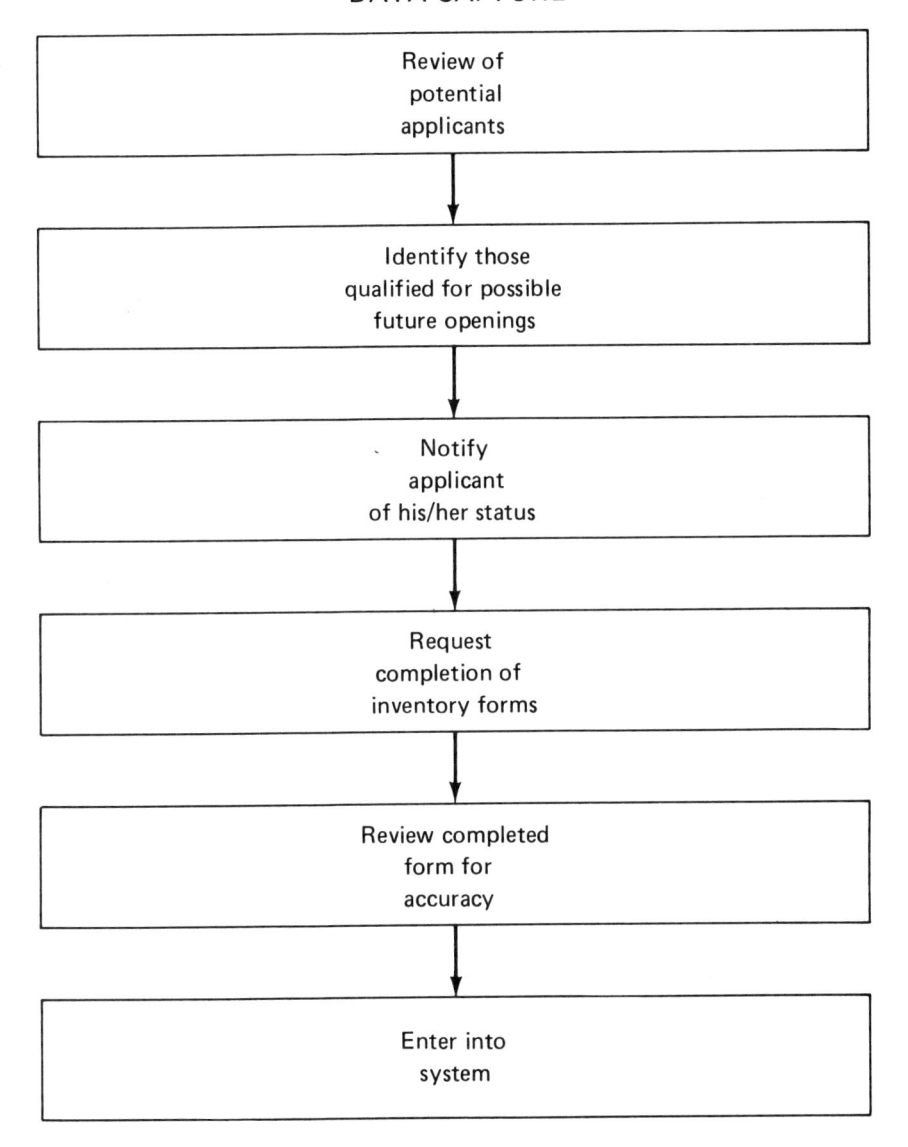

Figure 7-4

organization truly intends to "keep the application in the active file." Most applicants would be more than willing to participate in such a program. Even if contacted at a later date when a new position has been successfully located, this is always a positive experience. People like to be wanted and to have their skills in demand.

COMPETITIVE ADVANTAGES

This system allows us to continue to identify and retain information on qualified people. These are people who have applied to us for a position, and even if they find a new position, they came to us first. We have the date of application on file in our inventory file.

Many organizations are concerned, and justifiably so, with maintaining a professional image. Pirating (hiring away someone else's employee) is frowned upon, but within a reasonable time, say a year after the inventory is filed, we probably need to follow-up. We may want to send an enquiry letter or form (See Figure 7.5) to see if the applicant still wishes to remain in our active file, and if he/she wants to update any information.

This allows us to keep the file purged of anyone who is no longer interested in our organization. When doing external searches we are only contacting people who have indicated within a year a written desire to join us. Some people may feel that a year is too long—so be it. The follow-up can be run on a semi-annual or quarterly basis. Most applicants who are interested in our organization are certainly not going to mind our continued show of interest.

Those applicants who indicate on the form that their skills have changed significantly since first contacting us, may require some additional work. We may want to send them a copy of the skills inventory form and have them update it. If the system provides a turnaround document we may want to send a copy to outside applicants for update at the same as we do for our own employees, so that the material on file is kept fully up to date.

A competitive edge is a very real possibility for those setting up such a system. There is an opportunity to identify qualified candidates and keep them on record for future openings. These people are

QUESTIONNAIRE
OUTSIDE APPLICANT

To: From:

Our records show your name is on file in our skills inventory system.

Do you wish to remain active in this system?

    YES ☐   NO ☐

If Yes and there is a significant change in information submitted, please indicate and we will send you a form to update our records.

YES, A SIGNIFICANT CHANGE HAS OCCURRED. PLEASE SEND A NEW FORM. ☐

NO SIGNIFICANT CHANGE, AND NEW FORM NOT PRESENTLY REQUIRED. ☐

COMMENTS: _____

_____

_____

_____

DATE: _____ SIGNATURE: _____

Figure 7-5

normally lost to most firms, since they are looking primarily at present openings.

This type of system can reduce the lag lead time to fill an opening. Under standard procedures an opening is noted and a requisition is created. Those responsible for finding candidates must then make certain they understand the specification for the position, at which point an advertisement or other recruiting effort is undertaken. Information (résumés, letters, etc.) on candidates will arrive over a period of days or weeks. This information is reviewed and further screening interviews are set up. Ultimately, the most qualified candidates are sent to the requesting managers for further interview.

Using the skills inventory, the time needed for this process can be greatly reduced. When the requisition is received and a search of the internal file reveals no one, a search of the external files is made. We already have identified and pre-screened the people in this file. A telephone call can be made to arrange an interview with the candidate and the manager who has the opening.

In this instance the candidates can be meeting with the manager in a day or two. Without the intervention of the skills inventory, there are normally weeks or months involved before we reach this stage. During these weeks or months, the job may be in limbo with no one to perform it, and a loss is incurred.

It is assumed that there is a positive value to the organization when this task is being performed, and that when it is not being performed there is a loss to the organization. Speeding up the filling of the position decreases the loss. Those organizations utilizing such a system may find that over time they have significantly enhanced their competitive position.

8
EXTERNAL PURCHASE CONSIDERATIONS

MAKE OR BUY CONSIDERATIONS

We have several choices when it is decided that a skills inventory is going to be used. The skills inventory can be designed internally, we can purchase a package system, or we can purchase the assistance of an outside firm to develop a system for us. In each case there are pros and cons to be considered. The needs of the organization and the needs of its management team must be weighed.

DEVELOPING INTERNALLY

There are several considerations regarding the "make" decision in developing a system internally. One of the first concerns is to discover whether the organization possesses the technical capability to develop and implement a skills inventory system. If this capability does not exist, then we have to go outside and purchase it. In essence, we have to bring someone into the firm who is either an expert on the topic or can be developed into an expert.

This staff commitment may be of real concern to some organizations. What do you do with this specialist, or more probably, group of specialists, after the system is developed? If you have hired experts in the area, do you have a place for them in the organization when the task is completed? Today more and more organizations view the hiring decision as carrying with it a responsibility to the employee. In the past, employees might be hired to do a job and then released when the task was completed. This still occurs today, but at a reduced rate. More and more, organizations are assuming the social responsibility that many feel goes with the decision to bring someone onto the payroll.

Organizations have varying reasons for wanting to "make" their own skills inventory system. Many, by nature, have strong concerns about internal security. The information contained in a skills inventory deals with personnel related material on individuals which the organization normally guards very closely. Having this in the hands of any outside group or consultant can be a very disturbing thing for an organization of this nature. It goes against all internal policies, procedures, and the general psychological make-up of the management.

Another reason to develop your own skills inventory may appear after a survey of what is available in your particular industry. Management may not be satisfied with what is being used, or the "state of the art" of what they see. In some cases, one way to get what is desired is to develop it oneself.

Still another, and unfortunately a very common reason, is not taking the time or making the effort to explore other alternatives. Many people do not realize that there are other ways of getting a skills inventory system up and running besides doing it themselves. However, as systems are becoming more sophisticated, people are looking around and are becoming more aware of alternative resources.

PURCHASING A PACKAGE SYSTEM

There are many firms in the business of selling packaged skills inventory systems. These offer several advantages, since they have been used and tested with many other organizations. One item to check when these are under consideration is the past experience of several organizations. Preferably, these will be about the same size as yours, will be performing similar functions to yours and will have used this vendor's skills inventory system for a reasonable period of time.

Do not hold back on requesting references and checking them out fully. Find out whether the experience has been good or bad. Ask these references if they know of others who have used the system. Normally, the vendor is going to give you the names of people they feel will be positive, but every system has its strengths and weaknesses. It is much better if you learn about the weaknesses in advance to see if they are ones you are going to be able to live with, or if they are going to be crucial factors to your organization and management.

Another significant factor that a package system may provide is time. Development, particularly putting together your own system, can take months if not several years. One of the questions to ask is, how important is it to have the system up and running right away? Is management willing to wait a year or two to have a system tailored to its specific needs?

Most package systems can be in a place and operating in a matter of weeks or months. The forms are already designed, instruction packages established, computer program (if applicable) written, etc. This allows the system to be brought up very rapidly.

One very real concern that needs to be explored is the ability to modify the word package or system for your organization. A good package system should have some flexibility in this area. Unless the system was designed to be sold specifically to an organization almost identical to yours, there will be a requirement to modify accordingly. Tailoring of the system can make the difference between a good system that meets the needs of the organization, and one that falls into disuse and ultimate failure.

OUTSIDE CONSULTANT

There is the other possibility of using an outside consultant or team of consultants to provide the desired service. Some package system vendors provide almost an identical service. These are the ones that will analyze your organization and modify or adapt their system to fit your needs or requirements.

In the event a suitable package system with this type of service is not available, we may want to explore this other possibility. There are numerous systems consultants available to provide just about any type of service an organization can request. These services range from administrative support, through software support, and to hardware definition and development.

This allows you to define your skills inventory and contract for its design and development. Doing this requires a certain sophistication or ability within the organization. You have to have a clear cut idea of your needs, and you must be able to define what you want in an inventory system.

If a clear cut definition is not at hand, and you want to work with an outside consultant, you may want to take an intermediate step and arrange a small contract with a consultant to define in some detail the type of system the organization wants and needs. You may find that after doing this you have opened up some of the prior considerations of developing internally or purchasing a package system. A comparison chart is shown in Figure 8.1.

When a clear definition is established, and reduced to writing, and if you still wish to use an outside consulting group, there are other actions to be taken. The first is to solicit bids on the project. We normally want to get three or more, but there is no clear rule of thumb. It is best to contact all groups represented in your area that might be able to support your project.

Again, as with a package system, it is not just the lowest bidder that we are looking for. Cost is certainly a factor, but quality and competence is usually more important. Consultants can vary in this aspect and we want to be certain that the end product is going to meet the needs of everyone. There is no benefit in saving a few dollars and having a system that does not meet the organization's requirements.

WHAT VENDORS AND CONSULTANTS CONTRIBUTE

We have talked quite a bit about using vendors and consultants in supplying or developing a skills inventory system. We have touched briefly on some of their contributions. These were referred to as the benefits, positive contributions, etc. These groups normally provide some items that internal development cannot give us. Let us take a look at what these are or might be.

MAKE OR BUY COMPARISON

	Internal Development	Package System	Outside Consultant
1. Possess the technical expertise to develop	Maybe	Yes	Yes
2. Internal security	Yes	Maybe	Maybe
3. Avoid hiring someone or staff commitment	Probably not	Yes	Yes
4. Available systems not adequate for management	Yes	No	Maybe
5. Not aware of other systems development	Maybe	No	No
6. Time to develop system is excessive	Maybe	No	Maybe
7. Flexible in modifying system to fit the organization	Yes	Maybe	Yes
8. Sophistication to contract with outside vendors and consultants required	No	Maybe	Yes

Figure 8-1

The previously mentioned staff commitment will always be high on the list. There is no such commitment with vendors and consultants—at least their commitment lasts no longer than the contract. Also, time was mentioned as a factor. These services, particularly the package systems, can be rapidly installed. This avoids a prolonged waiting period to have the system up and running.

Many times you are also getting some other very important benefits or contributions. Up near the top might be ranked the concept of "state of the art." Most consultants and vendors have to be current with the product or service they represent. The systems field, being highly competitive, makes this even more necessary for those in the area. An obsolete product or service will soon find no takers in this competitive market. New innovations and advances quickly find their way into use.

Most organizations do not have the internal resources to keep up with the technical advances as rapidly as they would like. Those specializing in a particular field have to, if they are to remain in business and continue to grow. Many vendor packages automatically offer these new enhancements to their customers as they are developed and installed. This allows a skills inventory system to remain current with the inclusion of the latest advances, rather than growing obsolete and eventually having to be replaced by one which has kept pace with change.

Vendors and consultants usually have another very valuable commodity to offer. This is a breadth and depth of experience with skills inventories. They have usually experienced or heard about almost any problem that you may have or may encounter. This can save a lot of time and money. It is in a way preventive maintenance. Why learn the hard way? One of the items you are purchasing in this relationship is problem avoidance.

People who are marketing inventories or the related services have this experience or should have it. This is one of the concrete items you will want to look for when reference checking these individuals or groups. The more related organizations they have serviced, the greater the probability they have experienced any problem that may arise in their work in your organization. This enhances their value to you.

LOCATING VENDORS AND CONSULTANTS

This section is written almost with tongue in cheek. Many people in industry, government and education have little or no trouble locating vendors or consultants. On the contrary, their problem may be just the opposite, since at times, there almost seems to be an overabundance in the marketplace. Though this is true in actual number, it is doubtful that it is true about those that are fully qualified. The only true way to find those of highest quality is through a long and extensive reference check.

There are many ways of actually locating people to bid on a system for you. Excellent sources are usually found in most large accounting firms. If they themselves are not doing consulting, they usually know who is doing so in your area. Since these firms deal with multiple clients, they can make enquiries on your behalf to locate organizations of a similar nature that have found vendors or consultants. These are usually highly reliable sources of information, and many times will perform pre-screening functions before making recommendations.

Other firms in the industry, even though they may be competitors, are also excellent sources. Most competitors have established information exchange programs where vital patents or specific processing details are not involved. Information in the administration areas is usually exchanged freely. Those recommended will have experience with your type of organization.

Universities and colleges are another source of recommendations. In some cases people on the faculty may be engaged in this activity. If not, they can usually recommend people with whom they have had contact. They are active in professional organizations which have varied people in their memberships. Some of these are bound to be vendors or consultants in the area of your interest.

Often the vendors or consultants themselves are very good sources for others you may wish to contact. Part of their sales presentation deals with competitive analysis. They tell you who their local competitors are, and how well they stack up against them. If their presentation does not contain this information, it is suggested that you request it. This not only provides you with additional sources, but provides a technical education on some of the critical points with which you should be concerned.

These are but a few ideas on how to approach finding people to bid on your skills inventory. Once the word gets out that you are in the market these sources will seem to grow and multiply. You will probably find yourself on mailing lists and receiving enquiries for many years to come.

MAKING THE SELECTION DECISION

There are some very practical do's and don't's in making the selection decision. Many vendors and consultants are professionals in every way. This includes being professional in the art of making presentations and in selling their services. Do make certain you are getting what you want and need—don't be sold something other than what you seek. As mentioned several times already, do reference check thoroughly before entering into any contract or agreement.

Always look for a certain degree of flexibility from both vendors and consultants. Are they going to give you just what they have, or are they willing to modify their product or service to meet your needs? No two organizations are alike, each has its own character, style of management, and if you will, its own personality. Most skills inventory systems are going to require some personal modification to ensure that the unique nature of the organization is reflected. True professionals in the field will provide a certain amount of flexibility to accommodate these needs. If you are lucky enough to find exactly what you need, you are fortunate. Should you not, but find a vendor or consultant who will modify his/her system to meet your needs, you are also very fortunate. The end solution in both cases is a system that treats your organization as the unique entity it is.

Another area that should be explored is the type of technical support that will be available. The first concern, of course, is the technical support that will be available when the system is first installed. There are many questions to be answered in this area. Will they be sending a team to assist, one person, or no one? What is the background of those who will be present? How long will this assistance be available during start-up? Your own in-house technical people can probably evaluate this part of the proposal for you. It is wise to include them at the very beginning of any proposal to provide the necessary counsel and guidance in this area.

Your concern with technical assistance should not stop with getting the system up and running. If it is a computer based system, you know it will change over time. New equipment will be available, systems changes will be forthcoming. Will you be readily able to take advantage of these? What will the additional cost be? Do you receive changes automatically? These are but a few of the questions in this area that must be confronted at some time. It is best to handle them in the proposal stage. Again, your own technical people can be of tremendous help in reviewing, analyzing, and guiding you in this area.

Many people pursue the technical support in great detail, but what about the administrative support? Who will revise the instruction package? Who will train managers and supervisors in the use of the system? What about actually running the searches and conducting the periodic and annual updates? Does the outside service offer to perform any or all of these types of services? Questions of this nature also should be handled during the proposal stage.

This proposal stage can be critical for your organization. You want to make certain that all your needs and requirements are identified to the vendor or consultant. Be certain that all your questions are fully answered and documented. Do not hesitate to request that promises be put in writing, even at this stage, before you get to the contract.

If you are dealing with a firm of any size, you may very well be dealing with a sales representative. Chances are good this is not the same person you will be dealing with when the system is operational. The old saying that "promises are only as good as the paper they are written on" rings true. It may take a little bit of time to reduce things to writing at this stage, but everyone involved will be grateful later on, since it avoids many problems. This goes not only for you, but for the vendor or consultant with whom you may be dealing. Often customers have misinterpreted or read into a sales presentation things that were not there.

PREPARING THE CONTRACT

When all proposals have been reviewed and one has been decided upon, another phase comes into play. This phase involves preparation of the contract. In some cases, the vendor or consultant may have already drawn up such a document. Regardless of who initiates the document, there are certain points you will want to be sure are covered.

The document must be reviewed by your own legal staff. Identifying the points you want included provides them with some assistance. It gives them a framework and pinpoints significant items for them to review. They still provide a vital role in being sure that details are properly spelled out, and that the contract is within organizational policy, and proper legal format. If you are a small firm and do not have a legal staff, it would be advisable to seek qualified counsel. The dollars spent are usually a small fraction of the total contract. You further insure that you will receive the end product you want, plus the fact you have provided for your own peace of mind in knowing that all bases have been touched.

There are many things that may be included in the skills inventory contract. Each organization has its own requirements and variations. A list has been provided to serve as a starting point. The following are some of the items you may wish to consider for contract purposes.

Dollar Amount

Most contracts automatically pick up the dollar amount that is to be paid, but there are still many variations involved in this. The amount may be a lump sum or a per diem (per day) rate. In either case there are a number of questions you will want to explore. Does the lump sum cover everything? Are you to pay expenses—mileages, photo copying, etc., or is this included?

One particular problem can occur in dealing with expenses. If the handling of all expenses is not detailed you may want to spell them out. There probably should be a cap put on expenses. For instance, "covered expenses will not exceed two thousand dollars," or something to this effect. Expenses can mount up fast if a limit is not established. You do not want to wind up spending ten thousand dollars on the product, and get a similar size bill for travel, lodging, etc., for a team of specialists.

The same considerations apply if you are considering per diem rate. Is there a limit on this? How many people are involved in receiving it? These are items you want to have spelled out. The rate quoted may be five hundred dollars a day per team member. If there are two team members that is a thousand dollars, and ten would be five thousand. Several days at these rates can soon mount up to a sizeable sum of money.

Milestones and Measurable Goals

Targets and due dates are easy to promise, but sometimes hard to meet. Someone in the organization has the task of overseeing the system implementation. Assume the project is to take two months to implement. After six weeks, everyone will assume that the project will be completed in another two weeks, and the system will be up and running. Something may have occurred earlier in the system implementation that will ultimately cause the project to be slipped by several weeks. Often this is not communicated until the due date is past, and the person overseeing the operation winds up finding excuses after the fact.

This type of occurrence can be embarrassing to everyone involved. It can also quite easily be prevented. One way of doing this is to put a requirement in the contract for a milestone chart. This will list items that must occur by a specific time for a skills inventory to be up and running on schedule. For instance, the computer program must be up and running for machine run forms to be created. The forms must be created before they are sent into the field for the employees to complete. The employees must complete these before the skills data are input to the system. Should any part of this sequence break down, there will be a time lag equivalent to whatever it takes to fix the problem. If this time cannot be made up by some future date in the implementation process, the entire project will slip by approximately that period of time.

A milestone chart can be laid out showing the stages that must be accomplished (See Figure 8.2). This forces everyone involved to determine if the completion date agreed to is realistic. As the steps that must be accomplished are spread out, any major gap or overlap becomes readily apparent. Assuming that there is agreement as to the functions and the respective time frames, we have a very effective follow-up tool. For example, after week number one we can check to see if the computer program is on schedule. By week number two the forms should be prepared and distributed. When these items do not occur, we know the schedule is slipping and by how much.

Completion Time

The milestone chart helps us firm up the completion date. It gives us a very real target and a way of checking prior to this time. The importance of meeting this deadline may or may not be a critical factor. Does something bad happen if we are two weeks late? Three? Four? By the same token, does something good happen if the system is up and running a week early?

The answers to these questions can determine how we write this portion of the contract. If completing the project is critical for any reason, we may want to include a performance clause in the contract. This can be based on a negative or positive incentive. We may want to provide a penalty if the date is not met, or a bonus if it is completed early.

One concern in placing any type of performance clause is the concern with quality. Quality control must be very carefully managed to insure that corners are not cut to achieve the bonus or avoid a penalty. Again, the determining factor should be the impact or benefit derived from exactly meeting the target date involved.

MILESTONE CHART
SKILLS INVENTORY SYSTEM
IMPLEMENTATION

Task	Week 1	Week 2	Week 3	Week 4	⟶	Week 8
1. Initial computer program	⊢⊣				⟿	
2. Forms prepared and distributed		⊢⊣			⟿	
3. Employee completes forms		⊢——⊣			⟿	
4. Completed data is input			⊢——⊣		⟿	
⋮						
10.						

Figure 8-2

Technical Assistance

When we discussed the proposal stage, the subject of technical assistance was explored. This should also be included in the contract. Too often, the only portion that is spelled out, if at all, is that dealing with initial setting up of the system and getting it running. There is a very real consideration to be made in the type, amount, frequency, etc., in supporting the system later on.

First, we have to get the system operational. Here we are interested in such factors as the type of support we will receive, the qualifications of those involved, how long they will be working for or with us? Who will determine when their duties have been satisfactorily completed? These are just a few of the general questions that must be resolved. The technical people in your organization are usually the ones to handle this part of the contract.

They also should review another very important part of the contract regarding the type of technical support that will be required to continue to support the package over the years. What about modifications? Assuming a computer based system, who will make any future program changes? Will we be advised of technical enhancements to the system we purchased? How will they be processed? Who will install them? There may be more questions and details that need to be analyzed and spelled out in the continuing support area, than in the support required to bring the system up.

Future Support of the Management System

We often consider the computer or processing portion of the system and forget about the administrative or the management part. This can be just as important to a smooth and effective skills inventory. Here we are dealing with items such as the instruction guide or manual, the input forms, the output forms and reports, etc.

The first concern is with what is to be provided for start-up. Will the vendor or consultant supply manuals, forms, and other necessary material? Will a master be supplied and printed by the organization?

Is there a recommended printer or supply house? Most of these items are negotiable and can easily be written into the contract to handle the start-up phase.

After this phase, the item of major importance is handling the management system over the long term. Who will supply the materials? What about revisions, will the vendor or consultant arrange for these, or is the organization responsible? What about an enhancement to the processing system—will this require a change to the management system? These are but a few of the questions and problems that come up during this later period.

It is wise to reduce this to writing. Define all aspects of what you want and need. Have your own technical people involved in this as well. They can point out possible or probable changes in the processing system which can have an impact later.

Results of Detailed Contracts

Often people are afraid that the vendor or consultant will find this type of activity offensive. On the contrary, many welcome having points clarified. They cannot keep their reputation and business if their customers are not satisfied. You are letting them know "up front" what you expect. They can then quote you a fair price for the service they provide, and let you know what cannot be provided. In this way there are no surprises and no hard feelings.

If there is a service they do not provide, it can be discussed and the problem mutually resolved. Nothing ruins a business relationship faster than two different and opposing sets of expectations. When these are not met someone feels he/she was treated unfairly.

This can also go a long way toward assuring a firm contract price. Some vendors and consultants may underestimate or over-estimate the work involved. This is often not the fault of any specific individual. It is the lack of communication between the parties involved. It is difficult to go back and make adjustments at a later date. The detailed contract avoids this because all major items have been identified and spelled out. No one is asking for anything more or less than what both parties have agreed to in writing.

As was noted earlier it is good to have an attorney review the proposal in detail. It might also be a good idea to have the attorneys of both parties present at the signing of the contract. This formalizes the process and ensures that both sides have availed themselves of legal counsel and review.

9
COMBINING INTERNAL DESIGN WITH EXTERNAL PURCHASE

OPTIONS

There are a number of systems-options. Just as with other decisions, things are not always black and white, good or bad, right or wrong. The same problem can be solved by many different approaches. There is seldom one answer or one correct way of doing things.

We have discussed in some detail the various pros and cons of using vendors or outside consultants. This has been compared to designing our own system. Fortunately, or unfortunately, depending on how you care to look at it, these are not our only options. We have other choices besides developing, implementing and running a skills inventory ourselves, bringing in an outside vendor, or having the assistance of a consultant. These are definitely the major ones, but we have the option of combinations and mixes of these.

What else can we do to get a system and have it up and running as we would like? The first thing to do is to get away from the idea that the options are limited to just three approaches. They are only limited because we want them to be, or because we have not taken the time to explore or consider the alternatives.

All of us get caught in this trap. First there is a problem or an objective. Most managers pride themselves on being problem solvers and quick to respond to the situations they are confronted with in their environment. This same rapid response time that leads to success in everyday business, may be a hindrance in the creative process.

We too often think of system work, in the general sense, as being pragmatic and without creativity. This is wrong, and we need to break away from a rigid thought process to come up with the type of system that will complement our unique organization.

CONSIDERATION FOR DEVELOPING OUR OWN SYSTEM

Many skills inventories are developed internally by individual organizations. One reason in the past has been that there was little on the market to choose from. This market situation has changed so dramatically that the decision-making process has become complex.

We previously touched on some of the reasons some organizations choose to develop their own systems. Let us look at this again, and go into a little more detail. In this way we can glean some insight into the hypothetical thought process which is occurring. We can also understand both the decisions that are made, and explore the options that are available for consideration.

An organization seeks to develop its own system for a wide variety of reasons, one being the philosophy of the company. This sometimes parallels what is referred to as the N.I.H. *(Not Invented Here)* factor. The management of some firms refuse to accept or consider systems or developments as worthy of consideration. This is the concept of "if they can do it, we can do it better." This may be true, but there is a cost in both time and money to re-inventing the wheel. Too often firms that need or could use a skills inventory go for years without one because their own is being developed. When it is finally completed and operational, it often is not any better than, or different from, similar ones in operation.

Every organization has the N.I.H. factor to a varying degree. If you stop for a few minutes and analyze your own organization, you will be able to point to areas where this has occurred or is occurring. Sometimes this is the philosophy of an individual or a department. Nevertheless, all of us encounter it too frequently.

Many people would suggest that the N.I.H. factor is only to be found in those organizations that are not forward thinking or inventive. This is really not the case. It is found in large doses in engineering and scientific firms, and those dedicated to advancement and research and development. It may be a manifestation of the inquisitive type that we see with the desire to do or develop something better than what has been done in the past—the desire to come up with a unique system.

Another area that was touched on previously is the desire for secrecy or security. Many organizations are very reluctant to deal with anyone outside, to the point where this almost reaches a state of paranoia.

The nature of skills inventory data itself directly contributes to this concern. Organizations are accustomed to guarding their personnel data, particularly when the information is spelled out on specific individuals. Almost all organizations will share or exchange overall statistical data such as the average salaries for a given job classification, the number of degrees in a given major, etc. These same organizations are most reluctant to release any information about a specific individual. They will almost never participate where employee names are to be given out.

This method of operation has several sound reasons behind it. First, most organizations have spent considerable time and money in recruiting, selecting, and training their staffs. If they are lost to another organization, there is significant time and money involved in replacing them. There is also the concern that they will take valuable knowledge with them that can aid a competitor. Even if it does not aid the competitor it still hurts the organization which lost it.

Another area of concern is consideration of individual privacy. This is an area where new legal interpretations are continually being made. If information on individuals were to be improperly handled or released, what would be the legal implications or ramifications?

Skills inventory files contain specific information on individuals. Searches are frequently aimed at producing candidate lists which identify people with selected skills. These lists must identify people by name to be of any use. Our next step with these lists is usually to select the individual personnel files for further screening and arrange interviews with selected candidates.

Many firms will only release this type of information to a vendor or consultant with great reluctance. Many others refuse to even consider letting anyone have access to this data. For some organizations, releasing this type of information to any outsider is a breach of their security requirements, and is a punishable offense.

Even for a liberal organization with no specific rules covering this situation, there can be concern. If nothing else, there is the concern with the legal ramifications if the information is incorrectly handled. There has to be a bond of trust built up with any vendor or consultant. Most secretive organizations fail to recognize that the vendor or consultant also has a concern in protecting the confidentiality of the data. Not only their reputation, but their business survival hinges on their ability to handle and protect the information entrusted to them. One mistake and they can be out of business.

Another reason some firms choose to develop their own system is that they are unable to find a system which is adequate. They feel the systems available for their type of organization are not satisfactory. This was probably true in the past, but it is becoming more difficult to justify each year. As more systems come onto the market, there is a greater variety and selection.

VENDORS

Many firms today sell assorted software packages. Included in a number of these are various personnel systems, and among these are skills inventory packages. Sometimes you must purchase the entire personnel system to also get the skills inventory, but in many cases this is negotiable and the inventory can be split off as a separate entity.

The design and modification of these packages can be a very important item. A system and related word packages should fit your organization. Is the vendor's system designed or modified to exactly fit your organization? You can usually tell this by reviewing the various sections, starting with the key word area.

The key words should be ones with which your managers are comfortable. They should not have to plow through terms that are unfamiliar or are never used by your people to identify internal skills. Test the system by circulating it to your managers (See Figure 9.1). If the package is acceptable, consider it as one of those to be

SKILLS INVENTORY VENDOR REVIEW

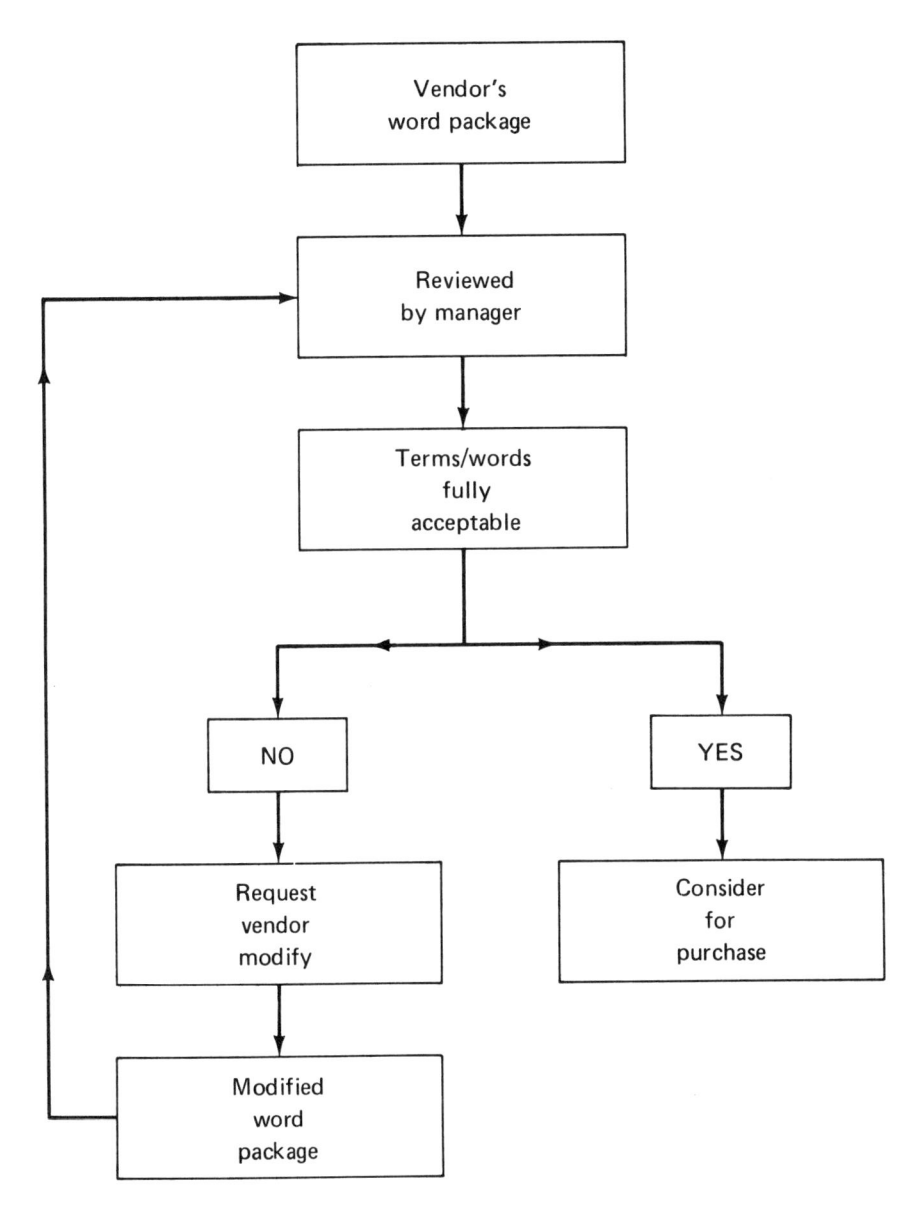

```
         ┌─────────────────┐
         │    Vendor's     │
         │  word package   │
         └────────┬────────┘
                  ▼
         ┌─────────────────┐
   ┌────▶│    Reviewed     │
   │     │   by manager    │
   │     └────────┬────────┘
   │              ▼
   │     ┌─────────────────┐
   │     │   Terms/words   │
   │     │      fully      │
   │     │   acceptable    │
   │     └────────┬────────┘
   │         ┌────┴────┐
   │         ▼         ▼
   │      ┌────┐    ┌─────┐
   │      │ NO │    │ YES │
   │      └──┬─┘    └──┬──┘
   │         ▼         ▼
   │   ┌─────────┐  ┌─────────┐
   │   │ Request │  │Consider │
   │   │ vendor  │  │   for   │
   │   │ modify  │  │purchase │
   │   └────┬────┘  └─────────┘
   │        ▼
   │   ┌─────────┐
   │   │Modified │
   └───┤  word   │
       │ package │
       └─────────┘
```

Figure 9-1

reviewed for purchase. Should it not be, ask the vendor if they will consider modifying it to meet your requirements.

Too often we just reject the packages without giving the vendor an opportunity to modify them. Making this type of decision might depend on the number of vendors who are bidding on your project. If there is an adequate number with totally acceptable packages, you may not need or want to take this additional step.

In the event you have not found numerous systems that perfectly fit your own requirements, the modification route may be a viable option. The vendor may gain in several ways by considering your request for modification. In the first place, there is the opportunity to receive your business. Secondly, you are probably not the only firm who would be interested in such a system. Other organizations in identical or closely related types of work would have the same requirements. Having the modified package to offer would probably enhance the marketability of their product.

CONSULTANTS

They differ in this instance from vendors in that they are not selling a pre-designed system. Their value is in having assisted in setting up numerous systems over a period of time. They are going to take the best parts of a number of different systems and incorporate them into a system for your organization. Again, you want to thoroughly review all word systems with your management to ensure direct applicability to your organization.

Making modifications with a consulting group should be of little or no concern. Part of their charter is to design a system to meet your needs based on their past experience and expertise. One of the concerns, or at least a consideration, is the time and cost of putting a system together in this manner.

A package system can be installed rather rapidly, since it has been developed and used many times. A consultant is going to select "building blocks" from various sources and construct a system for you. The time involved in doing this can be greater, which will lead to greater cost.

VENDOR/CONSULTANT

We have just looked at vendors and consultants as they relate to a skills inventory system, but it must be understood that this review has been an ideal definition. In actual practice the clear-cut separation seldom exists.

Most vendors are flexible and are deeply into consulting aspects of the business. Many consultants have favorite package systems, or soon develop ones of their own. In past discussions the terms "vendors" and "consultants" have sometimes been used interchangeably. This gives a much more realistic picture of the sources you will be dealing with.

ALTERNATE CONSULTANT USES

There are other ways of using consultants than having them design a system for you, and these should be explored. Many organizations, both large and small, lack the technical expertise to evaluate their skills inventory needs and requirements. They need someone who can come in, study their operation and make appropriate recommendations.

In this case, there is no intention of bringing the consultant in to design a system. He/she is being hired to evaluate the work of other vendor/consultants. It is their task to review outside packages and recommend the ones that would be most appropriate.

Their assignment can be to evaluate all or any part of the skills inventory. Suppose a computerized system is being considered. Your organization may have excellent technical people who can evaluate the data processing portion of any package with no difficulty. At the same time the organization does not possess a strong management systems group. The consultant may be valuable in reviewing everything other than the data processing portion, thus, focusing his/her efforts on the management system aspect.

Again, consultants vary in strength and experience. When selecting one for this type of review, we want to know if they have had specific background in this area of activity. References should also be reviewed and checked out. What is expected should be spelled out in writing, agreed to by all parties involved, with the end product being a signed contract.

JOINT VENTURE POSSIBILITIES

Not finding an inventory system that fits your organization or even comes close does not rule out the use of a vendor or consultant. If every avenue has been explored and a system for your particular type of firm does not exist, you may have discovered a potential market. You want and need a skills inventory system, so others in your field must have similar requirements.

A certain amount of extra effort is required to modify an existing system or to design a system for a new group. Extra time and additional testing will be required to identify the new requirements that must be met. Once these are met, the modified or new system has additional value to everyone involved.

If you serve as their testing ground, you also serve as a reference to the usefulness and accuracy of the system. Often your own people will be involved in design and development. Your investment includes possibly three different factors—special system testing, testimonial to systems usefulness, and possible design and development input.

Some vendor/consultants are interested in entering into a joint business venture based on your ability to attract new clients. Do not down play your value, particularly if you are a pilot organization. The joint venture arrangement can be favorable to both parties. You are providing a very valuable testing ground, and can verify to others in your industry the value and accuracy of the system.

The terms of any venture of this nature should be worked out prior to entering into the final contract with the vendor/consultant. If you have done your homework you are aware of what systems similar firms in your industry possess. If there is nothing, and you are pioneering a new market, discuss this with the vendor/consultant. Get it out on the table early, and if both agree, provide for it in the contract. Instead of being an expense, your skills inventory may become an income producing item.

WHAT LEVEL OF ORGANIZATION INVOLVEMENT?

One of the considerations that must be taken into account in dealing with vendor/consultants is what level of involvement the organization wishes them to have during and after the project. This boils down to what portion of the work is to be done internally, and what portion is to be given to someone outside the organization.

There is a lot of hardware and software review which normally occurs prior to implementation. What the vendor/consultant will supply, and what the contracting organization will supply is usually reviewed in detail. This same level of attention is normally extended to the hardware portion in the after implementation phase. This is detailed in Figure 9.2.

Most people overlook the software considerations after implementation. They may include programming enhancements, but that is usually about as far as it goes. There is often no consideration given to the many other areas that must be maintained to ensure both the continued operation and the accuracy of the data being supplied. A few of these considerations are as follows:

Training

There must be some provision for training the people who will continue to operate the system. There will be a turnover of the people originally trained, and there must also be training provided as the system is modified or enhanced over a period of time. Those involved in assisting employees in completing the forms, those reviewing input, new managers, etc., will all require training. This will be needed not just when the system is installed but on a continuing basis.

126 **Planning and Using Skills Inventory Systems**

SKILLS INVENTORY INVOLVEMENT

	Vendor/Consultant Involvement	Organization Involvement
During Implementation		
Hardware	X	X
Software	X	X
After Implementation		
Hardware	X	X
Software	O	O

X = Considerable attention is normally given to these areas in contracting phase.

O = Often forgotten or overlooked in the contracting phase.

Figure 9-2

Documentation

All systems change and grow as time passes. The skills inventory is no exception to this rule. Documentation is required for reference by those using any system. The more complex the system, the less information an individual can carry in his/her head and the more important documentation becomes. As systems enhancement or modification occurs, documentation, if not maintained, becomes obsolete and useless.

Forms

Forms are significant in the input and output operation of any system. Their importance becomes even greater if a turnaround document is used. Forms are particularly affected by additions, modification to length, and deletions to data elements in the skills inventory. A change to one of these items can have a domino effect on the system.

Searches and Listings

When the system is implemented, there will be an on-going need for searches and listings. The more effective the inventory proves to be, the greater the increase in the requests for these products. Processing all requisitions against this system can cause wide savings in the use of the system as labor market activity changes. Search volume during periods of prosperity when job openings increase would go up accordingly. In large firms, additions to staff may be required to support this activity.

Updates

The inventory will remain current only as long as the updates continue on a regular basis. Information changes as people grow and expand their skills. Also, people terminate and new hires are added, requiring that deletions and additions be made to the system. Many systems require at least a major update on the entire file on an annual basis, with partial updates monthly.

The updating process can be another item which may require significant staff support. Someone must be responsible for receiving, reviewing, correcting, any input received, and reviewing, mailing, question answering, for the output. This area also has fluctuations in workload. These occur during periods of heavy turnover and/or heavy hiring when the need for support is much greater.

Who Will Provide the Software Service?

As indicated, many organizations will discuss the ongoing service with the vendor/consultant as it relates to programming support. They also will request prior implementation support in all software areas. However, other than in the programming area, software support by a vendor/consultant is often overlooked or forgotten.

Why not contract for ongoing training, documentation, forms redesign, or whatever is required? Why does the organization have to perform any of these functions? The answer is that they really do not have to. There are those who feel it is all right to have outside assistance in setting up a system, but after that it is the organization's problem to continue running it. This is not correct, and some of the more advanced organizations are getting away from this type of thinking.

Some are turning everything over to an outside group, and this includes performing searches and preparing listings. When you want a search or report you have a phone number to call to make the request. Possibly this is channeled through one area in the organization. This way the outside vendor/consultant becomes familiar with those authorized to request searches, and can retain control over the release of information.

Contact with the same person or group in an organization has benefits other than just security. These people learn the language, capability and limits of the system. Requests that are channeled through them are reviewed and communicated appropriately.

Another question comes up regarding the expense of this method.

Will there be a savings by performing this internally? Each individual system has to be reviewed and evaluated separately. There are a number of cost factors involved in retaining operational or administrative responsibility for a skills inventory system.

Each of the areas requires a particular expertise. To conduct the training requires a certain background and experience, as does designing, or re-designing forms, conducting searches, etc. This capability may be available internally. If this is the case, and if it is not being fully used at present, we may want to use it in support of the inventory. On the other hand, if it is not available we may find that it is less expensive to go outside than to hire and assign someone to this project.

Today, many organizations are looking long and hard at the implications of making a staff commitment. Specialists in some of the areas we are talking about may be difficult to locate. In most cases even after they are located there is not only the cost of bringing them on board and up to speed, but there is the problem of keeping them fully utilized. If the skills inventory does not use all of their time, there is the question of assigning other projects that will justify the overall expense. These decisions should all be reviewed and the most attractive options costed out. Only in this way can we achieve our goal of a cost effective skills inventory system.

10
THE IMPACT OF TECHNOLOGY

MANUAL OR MACHINE

One of the first considerations, after deciding to implement a skills inventory, is the type of inventory that is to be used. Will it be manual or machine? The size of the firm certainly has something to do with this consideration. Most firms with fifty or one hundred employees will probably not require a computerized system. Depending on the nature of the work they may not need a formal inventory.

An earlier chapter dealt with some of the details regarding organization size and the use of automation. One of the basic premises being that the use of computers increases in proportion to the size of the organization involved. This is very true, but there are some other considerations that we want to review at this time. In some cases, this may seem repetitious or obvious, but it is felt that we need to bring it out again before going into the related material presented in this chapter.

One very real consideration is the existence of internal capability of one form or another. A large in-house computer operation might predispose an organization to immediately take this route. As previously noted, this would be based on existing usage and availability of the equipment for skills inventory use. Related to this is the technical support on programming, systems design, etc. The more of this human resource that an organization possesses, the more likely it will be that the system will be developed and run internally.

One factor which is often involved has a psychological basis and is often discussed openly. This is the snob appeal of "keeping up with the Joneses" (or the organization next door). There is a certain status to having a computerized system. Many organizations will argue for months over going to a computerized system when one is not really needed. If the reasons are analyzed closely, it becomes apparent that the real reason is the status that is involved.

We are starting to find out that all business decisions are not based purely on the hard cold economics of the situation at hand. Business decisions are made by people with egos. It often takes a fairly large one to raise to the top of any organization. There may also be a proportional marketing relationship here. Smart sales people have recognized and catered to this fact for many years.

Take a few minutes and think of some of your own organizational experiences. Most people can conjure up numerous stories of internal battles for choice office space, major moves, or reorganizations which never took place because of a senior officer losing a choice window office with a view. Remember the applicant who turned down a substantial percentage salary increase because a parking spot with his/her name was not part of the bargain?

We can go on all day with examples of ego-based decisions and concerns in any organization. None are immune, nor are they expected to be. All are made up of people with traits common to all human beings. What is needed is the recognition that this problem exists, and frequently plays a role in the decision making process. To deny it is to deny reality. But for this fact there will be computerized skills inventory systems that could just as well be manual. They may be serving a very important non-monetary need in the organization.

The selection decision of using a manual or machine system may to some degree be made externally. A vendor/consultant may have solved part of the concern as to which method the organization will use. In the case of a package system there is usually no choice at all. The system has been designed to run in a certain mode. In the case of consultant reviewing options, he/she will usually attempt to review the alternatives and the related advantages or disadvantages of a manual or machine operation.

Even using a consultant does not preclude a management choice. First, the selection of the consultant by management is often based on how closely their mutual interests agree. A good consultant, who intends to have future contacts, is finely attuned to the direction and interests of management. What does this mean? It means that if management wants a computerized system, even if one is not called for, there will probably be a computerized system.

OPTIONS IN COMPUTER USE

Technology has dramatically changed, and is continuing to change, throughout the entire computer industry. A few years ago, the only way you could have computer service was to be large enough to purchase and staff your own operation. This was a major management decision to say the least. A large portion of the firm's assets would be tied up in the decision both now and in the future.

Not so today. A section or office supervisor may be as high as the decision need go to gain the benefits of computer service. It no longer has to be a major irrevocable commitment of present and future assets. There need not be specially built computer rooms with tightly controlled temperature and humidity factors. It does not require people with highly technical math or physics backgrounds to operate and keep it running.

An area can now be computerized with a simple monthly rental agreement. The advent of leased terminals has brought computer service within the reach of even small organizations. Most operate using a standard telephone instrument as the link to connect the terminal with the computer. This also means that an organization's location does not limit its use of this type of system.

Watching vendors of computer services points out the flexibility of today's terminal system. Many carry their own portable terminal in an attaché type of case. Their home office and central computer can be hundreds or thousands of miles from the client they are visiting. All that is needed is an available telephone to connect the portable terminal to the main computer. Setting up the entire system and being in communication often takes no more than a minute or two. They can proceed to demonstrate their computer system the same as if the main computer was located next door.

The mini computer has also had an impact on the market and the options to the skills inventory user. These are small, stand-alone computer systems that can be physically within the using unit. There are many advantages to having physical control over the input and output.

The user is not dependent on another unit or group to produce their product. It gives them control over both the management system and the data system.

To further clarify this, a system is composed of a management system and a data system. The data system is where the actual processing occurs (See Figure 10.1). If this is controlled by another unit or group, it offers that much more opportunity for something to go wrong or conflicts to arise. A group that controls both the management system and the data system can establish and carry out its own priorities as its goals dictate.

INTEGRATION OF COMPUTERS INTO SEARCH PROCESS

Historically, most large computer skills inventory systems probably had their origins on decks of punched cards. The information was keypunched onto various cards. Each card had a social security or employee number and a card number for control.

You knew that name, work location, and other vital information for any individual were on a specific card—say card number one. Also, that degree, major, college code, etc., were on another card—say, card three. Since each card contained a social security or employee number, the necessary information could be tied back to an employee. The activity involved to sort and prepare listings was time consuming, to say the least. Under anything but emergency type situations, an organization requesting a search had to wait days, if not weeks, to get the results back.

Those who dealt with this type of operation remember some of the problems that went along with it. One or two trays of cards would get misplaced. This left gaps on the search information, and often the report itself. Somebody would drop a bundle of cards halfway through, and the entire sorting had to be started over. Keypunch errors caused search problems and questionable reports. There were

SYSTEMS TRIANGLE

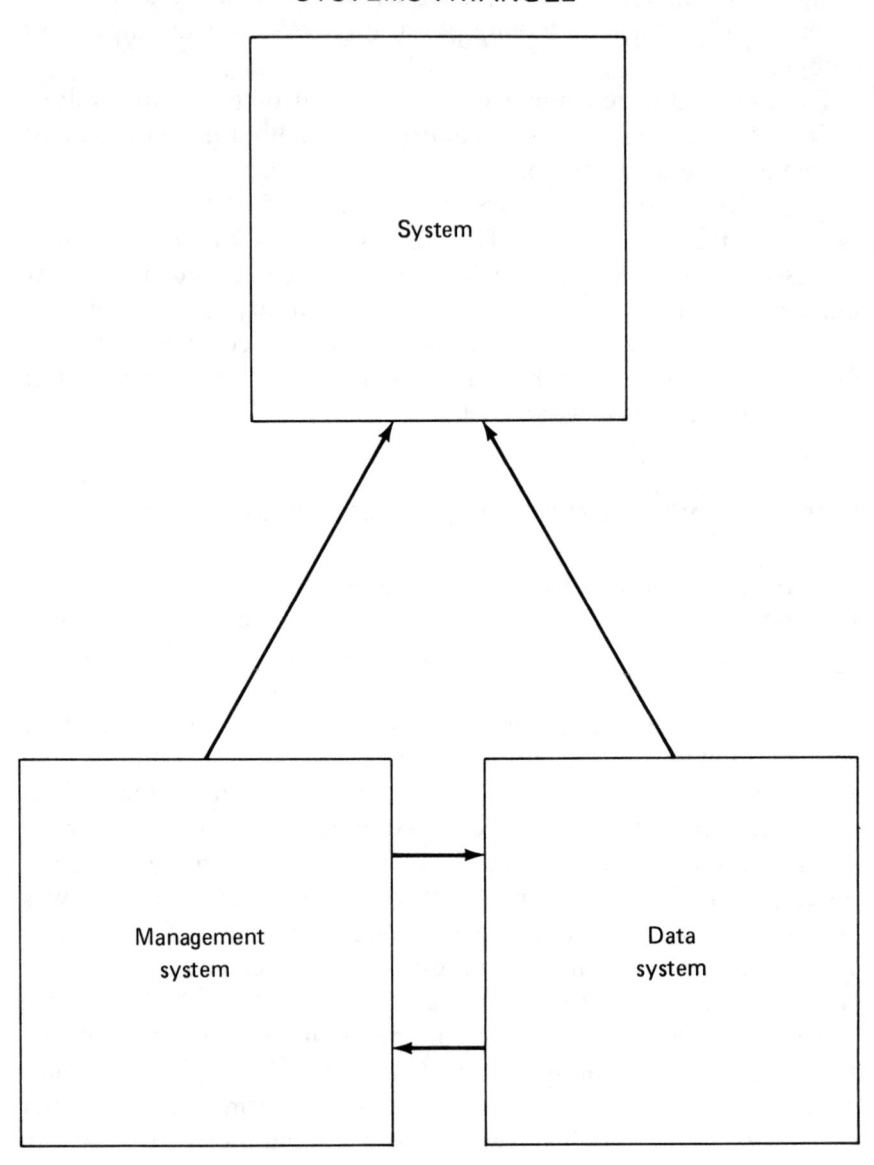

```
          ┌─────────────┐
          │             │
          │   System    │
          │             │
          └─────────────┘
         ↗              ↖
   ┌──────────┐    ┌──────────┐
   │          │ →  │          │
   │Management│    │   Data   │
   │  system  │    │  system  │
   │          │ ←  │          │
   └──────────┘    └──────────┘
```

Figure 10-1

many problems and complaints, but it was still better than being a large organization and searching the personnel folders by hand.

Computer processing progressed and helped to solve some of the problems. In the early stages, all of the processing was normally what is referred to as batch processing. This is where a number of items were grouped together for processing during the same machine run.

In this case, you might save up the requests for skills inventory searches and run them all at one time. This could be done once or twice a day if the volume warranted it. In most cases searches were run on a weekly basis. There would be very little problem if your search request came in on the sixth or seventh day. The turnaround time would seem rather short, since you would be receiving the response within a day or two. On the other hand, if you had a search request the day after the batch processing was conducted, your wait would be a week.

Batch processing had, and still has, some advantages. It is an economical way to operate the computers. Everything is run against the skills inventory program at the same point in time. Another positive aspect was that it was more accurate and posed a lot fewer problems than the straight card sorting procedures. There were still problems and the earlier systems sometimes relied on punched cards as the input and output media. This of course allowed for more rapid processing time, but presented many of the same card problems in the input and output areas.

Even when the computer systems completely converted from punched cards to magnetic tape there were still some problems, the major one being turnaround time. In some skills inventories this still occurs today as they are run on the batch processing system. However, we have discovered some ways of alleviating part of the problems created by the turnaround time.

One successful method was discussed in an earlier chapter. This is to print cross-reference indexes of the key words and other major identifiers. With this in hand, at least partial searches can be conducted externally to the computer. You may not be able to produce fancy listings, but you can supply the requestor with the names of those individuals who possess the skills he/she identified.

The external sets of indexes can be duplicated and sent to key locations. Some organizations have microfilmed them to make distribution even easier. The index system is even more effective if the system contains a well laid out biography (or employee resume). When a search of the skills inventory indexes produces a list of candidates, the biographies can be pulled and copies made. These copies can then be sent to the requestor. This allows him/her to view the entire background of the employee—or at least the background maintained for skills inventory purposes. Such a system allows additional screening without going through the process of pulling the employee personnel file.

USE OF COMPUTER TERMINALS

In recent years the availability and use of computer terminals has become widespread. It has had some impact on the skills inventory concept. Large amounts of data are still input through the batch processing method. Terminals however, have caused significant changes in some of the output methods.

Many users of inventory systems find terminals very useful tools to aid in the search/output aspect. Terminals can be placed at various areas where search requests would be received from line management. For instance, many personnel departments in large firms are decentralized to some extent. A personnel function may be attached to, or physically located adjacent to a major function that is to be served (e.g., accounting departments, manufacturing, engineering, etc.).

This type of close proximity allows for specialized service to the assigned group or department. The people in the decentralized personnel group become familiar with the unique needs and requirements of the people they service. They become familiar with all levels of supervision and the overall environment. Both supervisors and employees learn who to go to for assistance. This type of operation aids in overcoming the impersonal nature of large organizations.

These satellite sites or mini personnel departments may also be an interface for skills inventory data. In a large organization there may be ten or twenty such groups scattered around. Access to the system via terminals may be ideal in this type of operation. A terminal could provide search capability without having to physically go to a central location

We probably would not want to update files or add new employees through a terminal, as this is usually a slow way to accomplish this task. However, the system can be programmed to provide for this. Most often update information and changes would be collected, then processed through a batch mode at a central data entry unit. However, if the updates were not large in volume, it would be efficient to process via terminal.

This type of terminal use, again, raises the questions regarding security. If you have ten or twenty terminals, have you lost control of security? First, the information a specific terminal receives can be limited. For example, a terminal servicing the accounting department may be allowed salary rate information and other confidential material only for its own people. A special code can be assigned to each unit and individual on the file to control release of information. Most personnel units have this information in many different forms on their people already. The terminal is just providing the information in a new and different media.

We may want to allow full searches of skills categories, excluding classified information such as salary. This would allow a personnel unit to search the entire organization if necessary, for those who qualified for a specific need. In the event salary was also important the personnel manager of one unit could contact other units when a potential candidate list had been established. Searches usually are designed to identify five or ten of the most qualified people for any position. Getting rate or salary information from other units would be easier, since the numbers of people involved would be few.

Terminal inquiry and search is becoming more accepted in such areas as department stores, police agencies, credit bureaus, etc. There is always a certain amount of fear and reluctance when we confront any new concept or system. Certainly new problems, both anticipated and unanticipated, will result. These will have to be confronted and resolved. The terminal use provides a quantum leap from the old punched card system of a few years ago.

Terminals provide us with several advantages the old system did not, one of which is flexibility. Each search can be individually structured and designed. The second advantage, and maybe the most important, is turn over time. A terminal system can be designed to provide searches while you wait. Many systems attach medium speed printers to allow rapid printing of listings or biographies. Most managers or supervisors appreciate this capability. When they are in the decision making process, a wait can cause problems. Information is desired now, not the next day or even longer. The more they can depend on receiving the information rapidly, the more frequently they will rely on the system as part of their decision making process.

CHANGES IN TERMINALS

Terminals, like any other part of today's technology have continued to develop. Those who remember the first ones that came out, also remember the problems that accompanied them. In the early models making a connection to the main computer was almost a milestone event. This problem temporarily slowed widespread use.

Now we have fairly good reliability as well as options for transmission. Whereas the original terminals used a typewriter system, we now have the television style or what is called the Cathode Ray Tube (CRT). The CRT is ideal for viewing when a hard copy or listing is not needed. You can call up a record, review it, and no paper is involved.

This type of system goes a long way in avoiding the paperwork blizzard which comfronts most organizations. There are times when a hard copy or printed report is needed. For this reason most of these systems are tied into a printer. Simply by touching a print button or giving a related command, a hard copy can be had of what we see on the screen. This way paper is created only when it is actually required.

Another advance in terminal application has been in portability. An effort has been made to reduce both the weight and bulk of selected models. These can readily be carried in the same manner as an attaché case. As previously mentioned this is extremely useful for software salespeople, as well as others who are on the road and need access to computer capability.

The sound has been reduced significantly on some models. This avoids the necessity of having to isolate them in a terminal room. They can be operated on a desk top and not disturb other functions in the area. This is not only true for the CRT types, but for the typewriter terminals as well. New types of heat sensing paper make their operation almost silent.

Terminals are becoming more useful, since most people in the business world have had exposure and training in their use. For many years there was a certain mystique connected with them. the fact that they were tied in to a computer actually frightened some people, but that is no longer true today. People realize that a computer is simply another machine and not a mechanical monster.

A large part of the increasing familiarity with computers, terminals, and allied equipment is due to our school system. When these advances first came on the market they were, of course, new to everyone. The schools were often the last to get or use them, and any formal classes had to be provided by the manufacturer. Today this has all changed. Even young people in high school are receiving some exposure. Colleges and universities, as well as business and trade schools, all offer courses and hands-on experience.

Most secretarial classes provide exposure to computer terminals. There is a close correlation between the two. Since most terminals use a typewriter keyboard. Often we have a clerical staff that is most comfortable in the use of the computer. This is a major change from the attitude which existed just a few years ago.

In fact, there is a very interesting level of knowledge that seems to be making itself apparent. Young people coming out of schools and colleges have extensive exposure. The clerical and secretarial staff that has had recent training is also on board. Many have noted a gap in our management and supervisory areas. A number of organizations are beefing up their management training programs to handle this situation.

Progress on computer technology is being made on every front. Changes in machine languages and new techniques continue to make the use of computers and terminals more feasible. Figure 10.2 shows the progression from machine language to the spoken word.

Being able to communicate with a terminal or other related equipment by means of the human voice is not just theory. Certain applications of this technology are already in use. It will not be too many years before this can be used in the area of skills inventories. A manager will be able to verbally discuss his requirements and receive a verbal or written response. This will simplify the process and make the use and application available to a broader group of people.

One of the problems with computer technology is the complexity. In the early development only those with a strong math or science background could understand or use the technology. This has changed and is continuing to do so. When the computer can be used with the same ease as the telephone, even greater benefits will occur.

MINI COMPUTERS

Mini computers are very much what the name implies. Like a compact car they perform nearly all of the functions of their full-sized counterparts. Though smaller in size, advances in technology have packed them with some very powerful operating capabilities. Many of today's minis can out perform the full-sized computers of a few years ago.

In the past, only large firms could make the economic commitment to have a computer. As was previously noted, the price is now well within the range of most firms. The mini computer line is reasonable by most standards. It goes even further in making the use of the computer a reality for all organizations large and small.

Another benefit that is being derived from the application of mini computer usage is derived by the users themselves. In most large organizations all computers and all data processing have a tendency to be centralized. This meant that in the past all users had one source to deal with for their data processing needs. It was like having a monopoly, or the only store in town.

As the requirements on the single source became greater, it was hard to meet the needs of everyone. There were, and still are, more

The Impact of Technology 141

COMPUTER LANGUAGE EVOLUTION

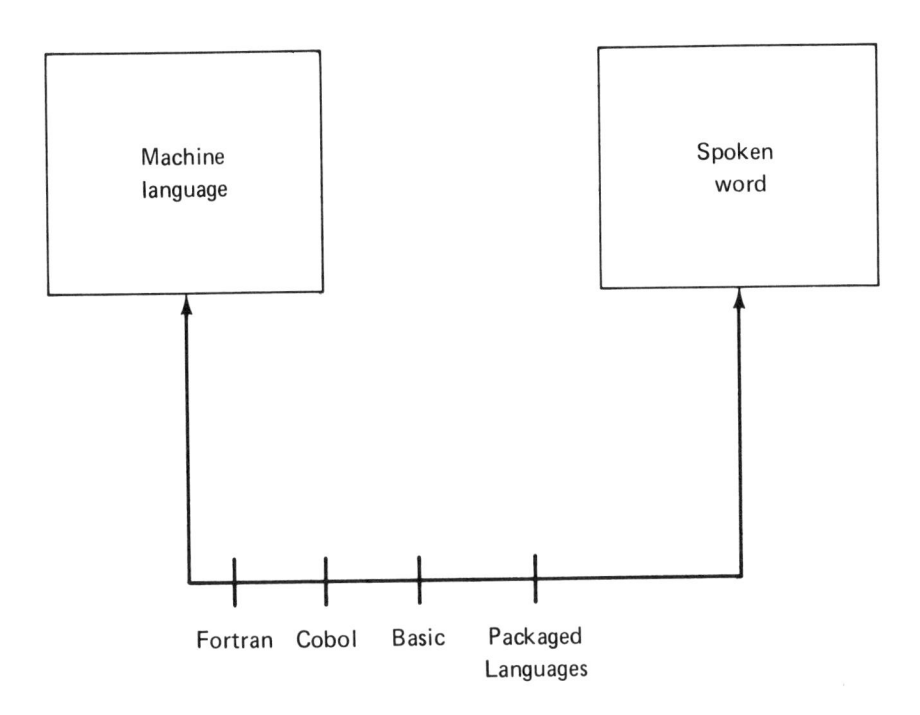

```
┌─────────────┐              ┌─────────────┐
│  Machine    │              │  Spoken     │
│  language   │              │  word       │
└─────────────┘              └─────────────┘
       ▲                            ▲
       │                            │
       └──┬─────┬─────┬─────┬───────┘
       Fortran Cobol Basic Packaged
                            Languages
```

DIRECTION OF DEVELOPMENT

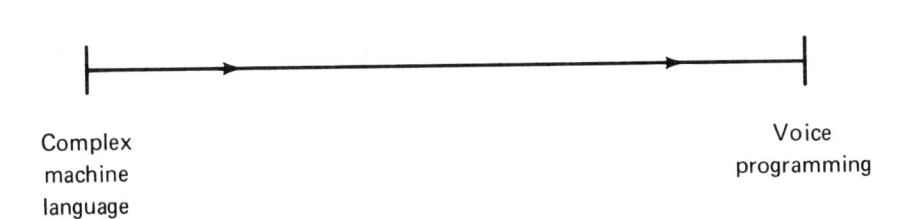

|─────────────────────────────────▶|

Complex   Voice
machine   programming
language

Figure 10-2

requests than resources to fill them. Users often wait until the last minute to make their needs known and then find they are at the end of a long waiting line.

To meet this type of situation priority committees and groups are often set up. These are aimed at determining which is the most important job and to try to make some order out of the large number of demands. Unfortunately, this type of activity does not seem to solve the problem. It is just a more formal or structured way to tell the user, "No, we can't help you."

In some ways the mini computer has allowed the user to control his/her own operation. Depending on how it is set up within an organization, it may put the operation back in the hands of the user. A central data processing unit may retain control of part of the system, but the input and output may come under the control of the user. In this case individual users can order their priorities rather than being thrown into a group with many others.

This has had some direct impact on skills inventory systems. Generally such systems are lumped into the computer work done for the personnel area. Except for legally required reports such as those needed to meet affirmative action commitments, personnel work is seldom given top priority. It seems that it is always bumped by reports for payroll, the controller, marketing, and other departments. Now it appears that with its own control, personnel may be better able to handle support requirements for skills inventory systems.

At the time of writing the use of mini computers is still rather new. However their popularity is such that most organizations either have them in use or are in the process of introducing them although in many cases who will control them, and how they will be used has not been fully worked out yet. The potential for more user control is definitely there. Most users will admit that they desire this. However, there are advantages to central control that cannot be overlooked. At present, different organizations have had different uses for this technology. It will be several years before the total impact has resolved itself.

MICROFILM

Microfilm and its various forms has been with us for many years. It has always had application where large numbers of documents are being used or stored, particularly if these documents are going to be referred to in the future.

Skills inventories have always had certain microfilm applications. Large organizations produce quite a bit of paper to support their system. The biographies alone are numerous enough to consider one or more applications of microfilm. If we consider using external indexes, this is usually another possible area.

The support equipment for microfilm has been growing and improving as it has with other areas of technology. The film is much clearer today and of better quality than was the case several years ago. Readers to enlarge the image are smaller, more compact, and of better quality. Reader/printers that reproduce hard copies, produce documents that closely parallel the originals.

Many have found that the addition of microfilm, particularly to the output part of the system, has some very real advantages. One of these is the cost and ease of shipping, where remote sites or distributions over distances can be reduced to a few ounces of film. If a firm has to deliver documents to another division hundreds of miles away, the savings can be significant. Postal rates and costs of all forms of transportation are on the rise, and microfilm continues to offer a savings option.

Some of the newer systems have combined microfilm and computer techniques to provide random access search capabilities. This type of system is ideal for skills inventory searches. Many are stand-alone units that take up a limited amount of room. When the search capability is combined with the microfilm it becomes a viable inventory system.

COMPUTER OUTPUT MICROFILM (COM)

Computer Output Microfilm (COM) has gone a long way towards keeping microfilm in the fore-front. This concept allows the computer to produce microfilm rather than a printed output. It aids in reducing the generation of additional paper.

There are several approaches to producing COM. Most systems operate on a similar basis. Within the computer is a video unit which displays a picture on a television type screen. Adjacent to this screen is a microfilm camera which takes a picture of the image on the screen. In this way no paper is produced, but the image is recorded on the microfilm. The entire concept of microfilm has been enhanced by COM. There are national and international microfilm associations that continue to grow and expand. Microfilm has been a vital link to skills inventories in the past, and will probably continue to be in the future.

11
COST CONSIDERATIONS

WHAT TO SPEND

Every system has a cost. Skills inventory systems can range from a few thousand to several hundred thousand dollars or more. This is a broad range and significant enough to send shivers up management's spine.

The size of the organization certainly has some impact. A firm with a hundred thousand employees would normally require a more sophisticated system than one with only a thousand. However, the most crucial factor is going to be not just size, but the skills mix. The greater the number of job classifications, the greater the need for an inventory (See Figure 11.1). The more technical the position or job classification the greater the need for an inventory. This is shown in Figure 11.2.

The target here is the diversity of skills. Large numbers of job classifications or technical positions indicate there are multiple skill categories. There certainly would not be this diversity in simple numbers of people. Two thousand unskilled laborers would not have the diversity of one hundred specialized scientists.

Another cost factor to keep in mind is what our needs will be in the future as well as today. Most prices tend to rise. We may know that we are going to expand our operation within the next few years. In our planning we should identify what our skills mix will be. If it, too, will change, this should be taken into consideration as part of the decision on the skills inventory.

Suppose a firm is engaged in a manufacturing operation. This

146 Planning and Using Skills Inventory Systems

NUMBER OF JOB CLASSIFICATIONS OF AN ORGANIZATION

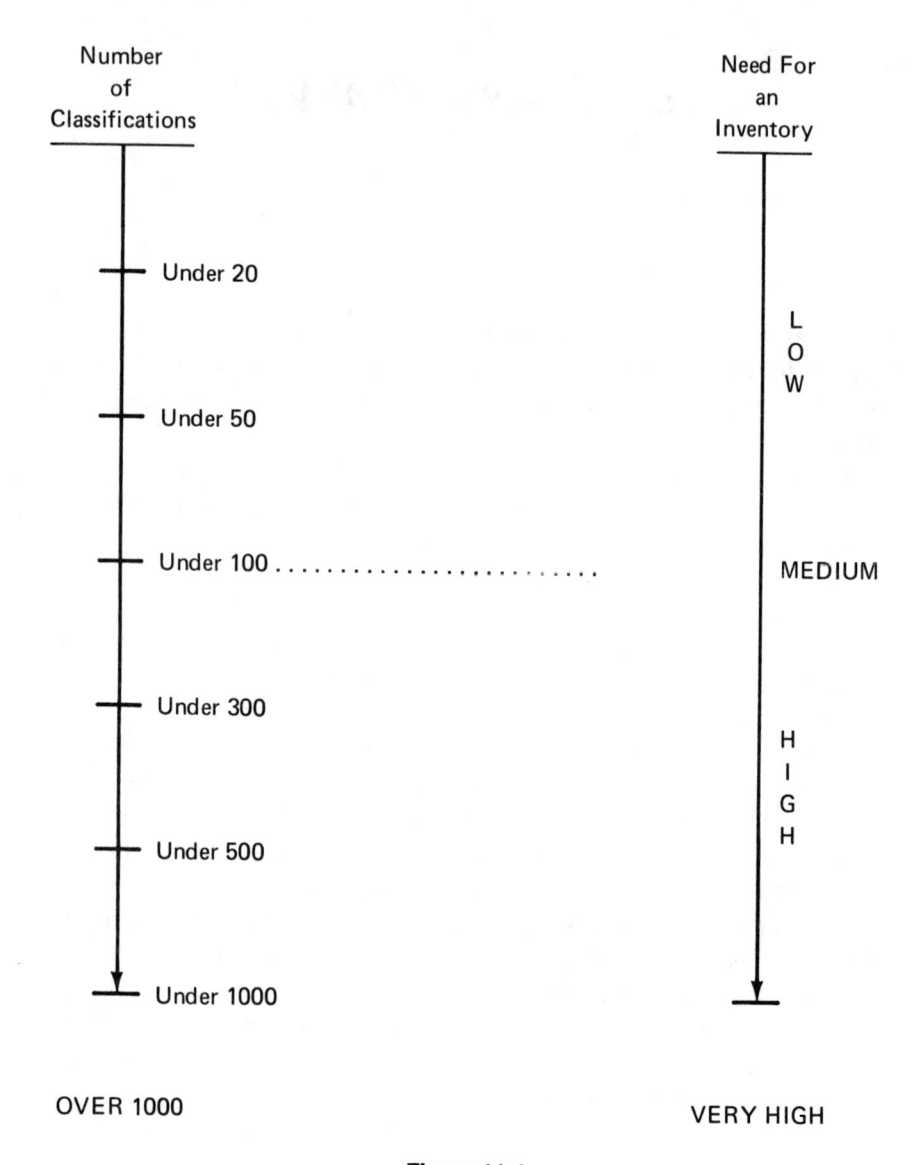

Number of Classifications	Need For an Inventory
Under 20	
	LOW
Under 50	
Under 100	MEDIUM
Under 300	
	HIGH
Under 500	
Under 1000	
OVER 1000	VERY HIGH

Figure 11-1

Cost Considerations 147

NUMBER OF TECHNICAL POSITIONS

Number of Technical Positions
— Under 10
— Under 50 ....
— Under 100

OVER 100

Need For an Inventory
LOW
MEDIUM
HIGH

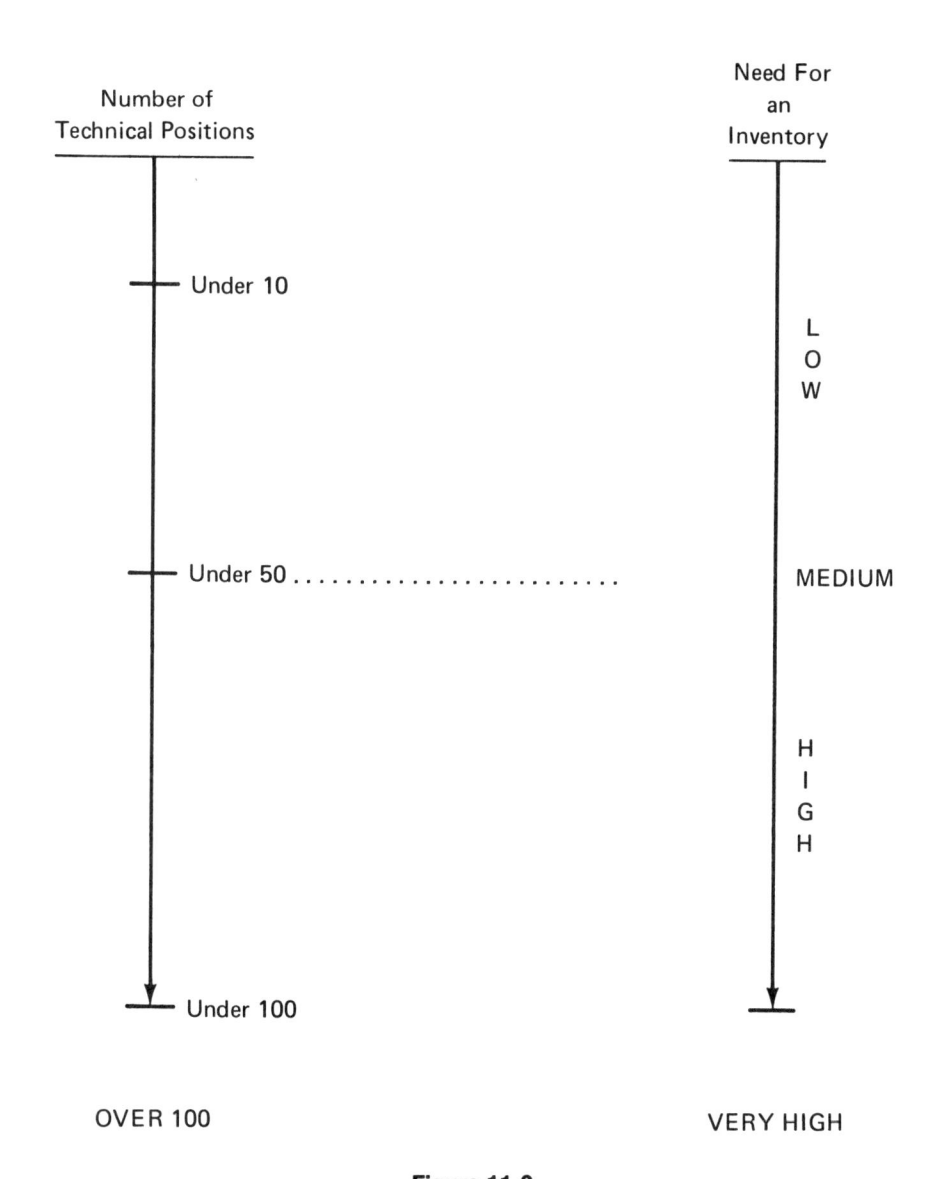

VERY HIGH

Figure 11-2

activity has been highly successful and expansion and growth have continued. Management has been reviewing alternate skills inventory packages to aid in making staffing determinations. What are the responsibilities of future mergers and acquisitions? Is the firm seriously considering buying out another type of business—diversifying? Where will the new holdings be geographically spread out? What type of corporate structure and control is anticipated?

These factors can have an impact on the type of system that is selected. Too often we fail to review our future corporate or organizational plans when making systems decisions. Cost and money allocation decisions are often mistakenly based on today and not on what is coming. It is the future that we are going to have to live in, not the present. The decisions which have impact today usually were made months or years ago in the business world.

Our skills inventory decision must take these factors into account. If future mergers are planned, we may be saving money by allowing for this expansion in the system design. Turning around two or three years from now and having to scrap the system, or make a major modification, will get us nowhere. Being able to absorb the new acquisition into the existing skills inventory system is a fiscally responsible goal. In fact, being able to provide for these additions goes a long way toward insuring a smooth merger overall.

CHANGING MOST CONSIDERATIONS

We keep referring to manual systems and machine or computerized systems. At one point in time there was a clear definition. Most functions were performed manually unless they passed a very strict cost justification procedure. Computers were expensive tools that could be run and operated only by highly skilled personnel.

You knew, almost without question, what was manual and what was machine processed. It was common for a contract request to come down from the sales department asking how many bachelors, masters, and Ph.Ds a firm had. This information was vital to the contracting parties, and had such priority that you scheduled everyone for overtime to search the personnel files. You knew the system was manual.

In addition, when such a common request was manual, you could assume that most of the other functions in the personnel department were manual as well. Taking this a step further, another assumption would be that few other administrative fuctions, with the exception of possibly the payroll area, were receiving support of automation. This was most often reserved for use by the engineering or scientific groups.

The decisions in these situations just described were controlled by the cost factors involved. Computers were expensive resources and were used accordingly. This meant that the engineering or scientific groups which contributed more directly to the bottom line were given what limited time was available, while the administrative units that are viewed as overhead or burden received little or none.

Today's situation is somewhat different. It is doubtful that the image of administrative units has improved. What has changed is the limited availability of computers as well as the cost factors connected with them. The "bottom line" units are usually being fully serviced and many organizations have time left over for others.

We have also discussed the availability to rent outside time from service bureaus. In most cases you can have a computer terminal delivered and installed which ties into an outside computer system in a matter of a few days. They will arrange to set up a data base, read your information in, and supply you with predesigned packages to prepare the necessary reports and listings. You don't have to be either a scientist or an engineer to operate this.

Charges for such an operation are not exorbitant. You rent the terminal on a monthly basis, and the storage and main computer time as you use it. In round numbers we may be talking in terms of under a thousand dollars a month. This is often less expensive than hiring an additional person.

Going back to our example of bringing everyone in the personnel department on overtime to conduct a search for the major degrees. How willing are people to even work overtime today? Many people, and particularly some of ths new entrants to the labor force, value their free time. Some unions have clauses limiting the overtime hours that will be worked, or giving the employees the option to refuse to work overtime.

Most personnel departments are non-union, since they are the ones who deal with the unions for the organization. Still, most contract benefits are extended to the non-union staff as well to prevent them from organizing. If a clause exists allowing union members to refuse overtime, chances are this is extended to the remainder of the work force.

These may have been extended theoretical examples, but they do make a point. Management may not have the options that it once did to get the job accomplished by manual means. Just to get the job done, period, may require that automated systems be provided.

We talked about the fact that using a computer system need not be the major financial commitment it once was. However, the cost of labor to conduct any type of manual activity is steadily on the rise. Not just the payroll dollar, but the "hidden" payroll as well. This being tax contributions, insurance payments, and the entire benefits package any firm must have to be competitive in the labor market.

In addition to this, today's labor force is more highly educated than ever before. There is a desire for challenge and opportunity. Few people today are satisfied with routine work. Most manual operations do not supply the challenge and opportunity that is being sought.

COSTS IN DEVELOPING A SYSTEM

As was discussed earlier, one of the considerations in developing a system is what internal capability exists. There is one cost if you have this capability internally. Should these people not be fully utilized on existing activities, your costs would be miminal to utilize the idle time. There are few organizations which can afford the luxury of such excess staff and still remain competitive.

There is another cost if you have to go outside the firm and bring knowledgeable people in to perform the task. This involves outlays for recruiting, selection, and all the other costs related to hiring and bringing someone on board. These costs are usually much higher than for the use of existing resources already available within the organization.

Staff costs are an increasing concern to most organizations. The best use of our dollar in this area is to insure there are adequate follow on projects for the individuals to perform once the major system is designed and running. We must remember that we are probably not hiring for the short term. In most cases, the individual or individuals will be around after the project is finished. It is not unrealistic to assume that, and idle time during the period of transition is also a cost chargeable to our skills inventory project.

The assumption that there are always more projects and assignments for both internal staff or those we are able to recruit and hire, creates another problem. Here we must look at the net worth of these other projects. This is an opportunity cost that we may be foregoing to design and develop the skills inventory. We must compare the alternate ways we could employ our resources.

The costs and alternatives in the design and development of a project are one of the major decisions for management. The diagram in Figure 11.3 shows some of the points that must be considered. As we have discussed in previous chapters the internal versus external, or inside versus outside is always paramount in the decision making process. Care has been given to place specific emphasis on this, since too often organizations do not recognize this option. By not doing so they drastically limit their choices in ths management decision making process.

COSTS IN DESIGNING INPUT AND OUTPUT

This is an area that is too often "shoveled under the rug" so to speak. We always emphasize the hardware and programming aspects of an automated system, but overlook the input and output aspect. This may be because we do not see extremely large dollars involved in this area. It just does not have the glamour of the automated or processing part of the skills inventory. Figure 11.4 shows a comparative analysis giving dollar expenditures versus the input, processing and output portion of the activities.

The tendency is to budget on the low side for expenditures on input and output. This can have a critical impact on our end product. The assumption here being that the end product is the use and performance of the skills inventory system. The appearance and structure (ease of use and application) of these materials has a very high visibility.

DECISION ON DEVELOPMENT COSTS

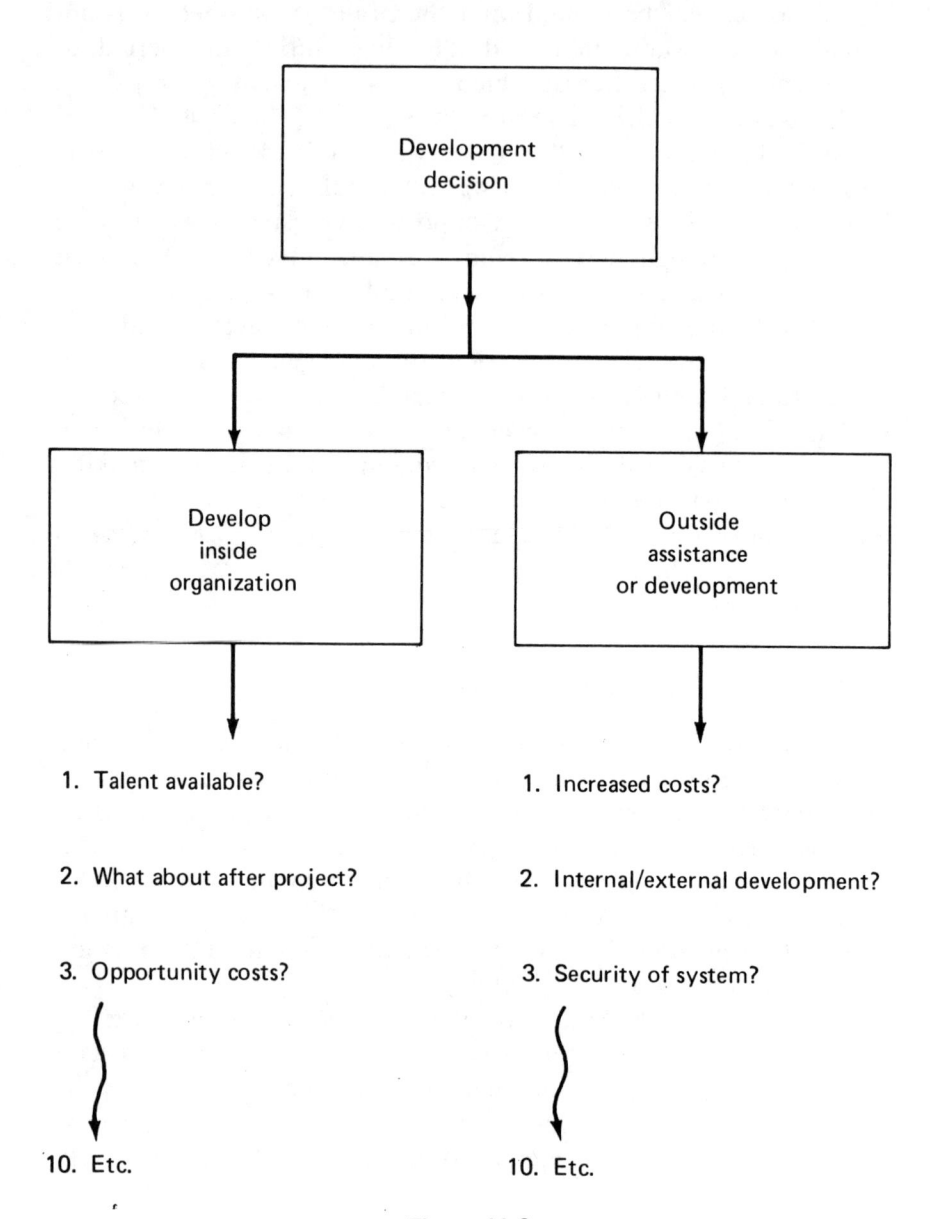

```
            ┌─────────────────┐
            │   Development   │
            │    decision     │
            └────────┬────────┘
                     │
         ┌───────────┴───────────┐
         ▼                       ▼
  ┌─────────────┐         ┌─────────────┐
  │   Develop   │         │   Outside   │
  │   inside    │         │  assistance │
  │organization │         │or development│
  └──────┬──────┘         └──────┬──────┘
         ▼                       ▼
```

1. Talent available?   1. Increased costs?

2. What about after project?   2. Internal/external development?

3. Opportunity costs?   3. Security of system?

10. Etc.   10. Etc.

Figure 11-3

Cost Considerations 153

DOLLARS
IN DEVELOPMENT

Consideration Given
Dollar Expenditures

Input (Includes forms, training, instruction package, etc.)	Frequently not sufficient
↓	
Processing (Manual or machine processing)	Normally heavy
↓	
Output (Listings, forms, turnaround documents, etc.)	Frequently not sufficient

Figure 11-4

154 Planning and Using Skills Inventory Systems

Let us take a look at some examples of what we have just referred to as "high visibility." Few people outside the computer room ever see the programs or the hardware. Management may have some brief exposure to this when the decision is being made as to which system to select. There are usually a number of salesmen, related briefings, and possibly visits to firms possessing similar systems. This aspect gets quite a bit of fan-fare, but is relatively shortlived.

On the other hand, take the instruction manual or the form that is used to guide the employees in completing the input to the system. Everyone sees and uses this, as they do the biography that is often produced from the system, or the listings of candidates that are run during searches. Employees are normally sent copies of their biographies, so they also receive a high level of visibility in the area.

Visibility in the processing portion by the employees and most of supervision is relatively low. The only time they really receive headlines is when this portion is malfunctioning. These are the periods when the "computer is down." This often receives publicity, but it is negative and the very type management wants to avoid.

The overall impact of visibility can be seen in the illustration in Figure 11.5. Here we can see the relatively high visibility for the input and output portion of the system. Most marketing experts will tell us that high positive visibility can have beneficial effects. Management is concerned about this as it relates to the skills inventory. If the employees and line supervisors view the inventory as a positive tool, there will be better response created in several ways. First of all, the employees will take more care in completing and updating their portion of the information. Hopefully, a much more accurate input resulting in a more reliable data base will result. Supervisors will receive an improved output from this alone. In addition, if the listings and reports they receive as output have been properly developed this has an even greater impact.

In most cases, expenditures are limited. The cost of a system is fixed by management within allowable ranges. This is required if there is to be a control system in existence. Figure 11.6 illustrates the fact that usually the expenditure "pie" is limited. A close look at the processing portion is one possible alternative to expanding the input

Cost Considerations 155

VISIBILITY
IN THE SYSTEM

Visibility within
the organization

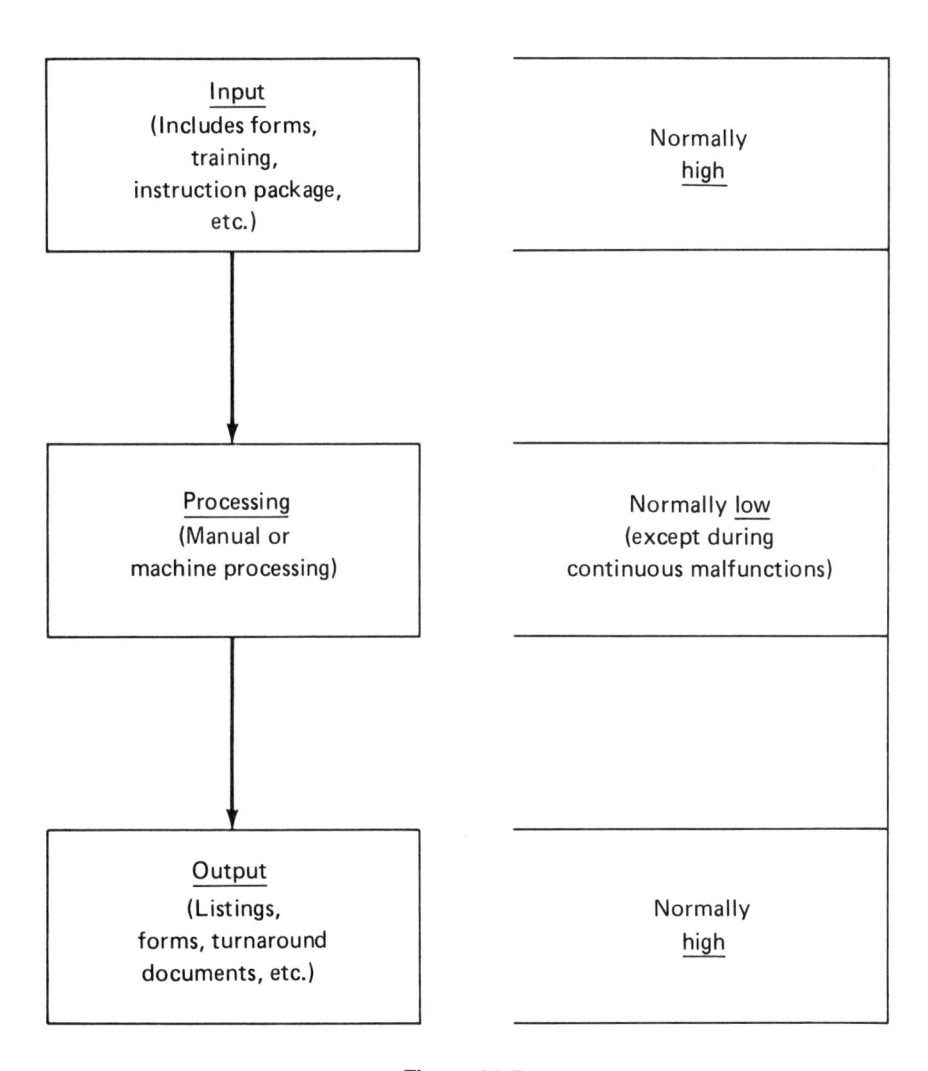

Input (Includes forms, training, instruction package, etc.)	Normally <u>high</u>
Processing (Manual or machine processing)	Normally <u>low</u> (except during continuous malfunctions)
Output (Listings, forms, turnaround documents, etc.)	Normally <u>high</u>

Figure 11-5

156 Planning and Using Skills Inventory Systems

EXPENDITURE ALLOCATIONS

Less for input and output

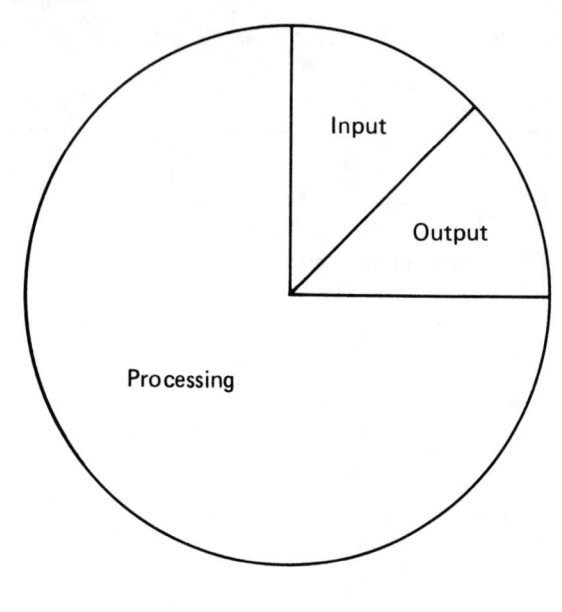

- Input
- Output
- Processing

OR

More for input and output

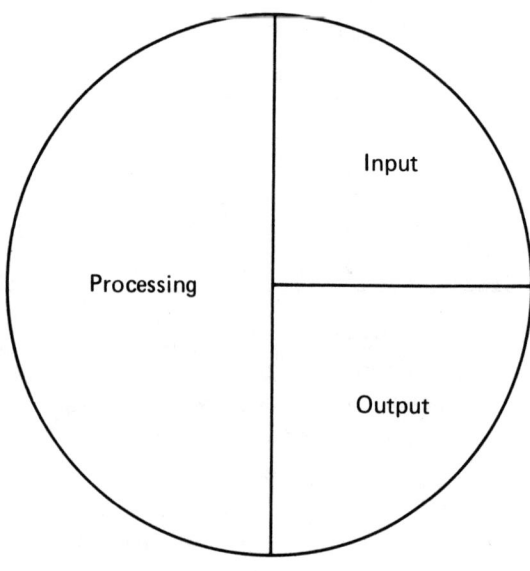

- Input
- Processing
- Output

Figure 11-6

and output areas. If the consequences of doing this are unacceptable then we have to go to larger overall costs or expenditures for the entire package (See Figure 11.7).

The point to keep in mind is to evaluate the processing portion carefully. Too often we buy an expensive "diamond" and put it in the processing section. A cheap "ring setting" is used for the input and output section. To carry the analogy a step further the stone often falls out and is lost, which makes everything worthless. If the money has been allocated properly in the beginning, many problems can be avoided.

COST OF COMPUTER PROGRAM AND HARDWARE

Once again, we are assuming we are dealing with a computer based system. This is most often the case today, and also usually constitutes the most significant or sizeable cost factor. Here we need to establish a setting for management's approach to costing out the factors involved.

To begin with, some explanation is involved. First of all, in this section, programming and hardware have been lumped together. Technically they are normally treated as separate entities. Programming falls into the software category, and is often under a separate management structure within an organization. Hardware will consist of the actual computer and the related support equipment. It, too, is usually under a separate management structure.

The question immediately arises as to why the cost factors relating to the two are seemingly being treated as one item? Do they not deserve or require separate treatment? They probably could be treated separately, but it seems more appropriate in this book to deal with them together. In fact, treating them separately for this discussion could not provide the detail necessary to do either full credit.

The other reason for treating them together is the management procedure for dealing with costs in this area. Most managers, outside of a few in the data processing area, do not have detailed knowledge of programming or the associated hardware. This is still a relatively new field, and we have many very good managers who have at the

158 Planning and Using Skills Inventory Systems

EXPANDED EXPENDITURE ALLOCATIONS

Option of increasing expenditures and overall costs

Input

Output

Processing

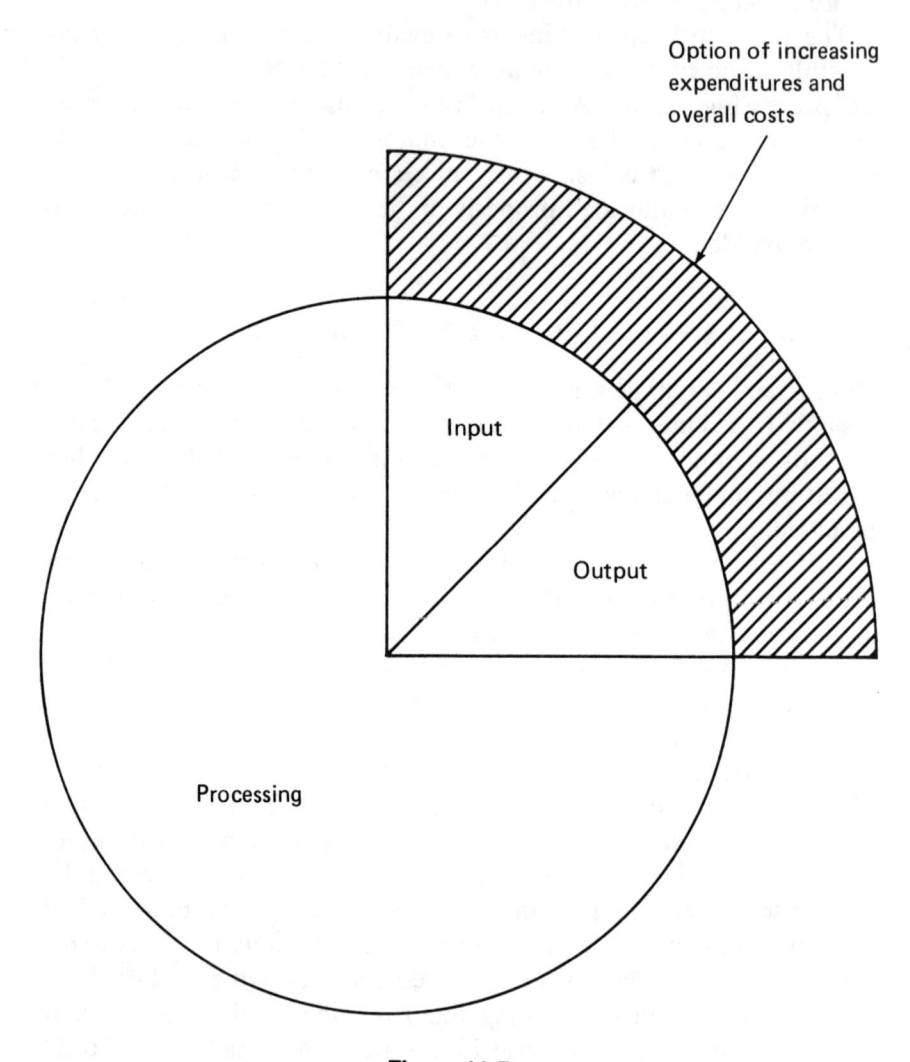

Figure 11-7

most only passing knowledge of the subject. Sure, many have spent several weeks in a seminar beefing up on computer technology, have, even taken a university course or two in it, and have toured a local facility. This has not made them experts, or even close to it, and most will readily admit this.

It will probably take a period of time before most organizations have the opportunity to fully bring all managers to the desirable level of data processing knowledge. As we mentioned earlier, most colleges and universities are now making this part of their curriculum. This will help, not necessarily the present generation of middle to upper managers, but those in the future. As data processing departments and groups are starting to stabilize, the training program of rotation from other areas is becoming more realistic. Still, the technical nature of the work continues to pose certain limitations.

This discussion has laid the groundwork to review what happens regarding cost decisions in this area. It points out that most managers must rely on their technical experts in the programming or hardware areas. This somewhat limits the latitude for discussion and decision making, since only a few managers involved will be technical experts. Today the average manager is still confronted with too much unfamiliar technical data when entering into the data processing realm, but this situation is changing rapidly and probably will not be a problem within the next decade.

COSTS RELATED TO PILOT TESTS

Another step in a skills inventory system, whether it is internally or externally provided, is a pilot test. This was discussed earlier in another context. Here we are looking at costs, and Figure 11.8 was designed to give some insight into the considerations involved.

Pilot testing consists of running the system using a small number of people. This group should be representative of the population of the organization. It should include people of all skill levels that would be included in the fully operational skills inventory systems which is to be used. This type of testing allows for optimum systems design. If properly designed, it allows for tests of various innovations

COST RESULTS OF PILOT TEST

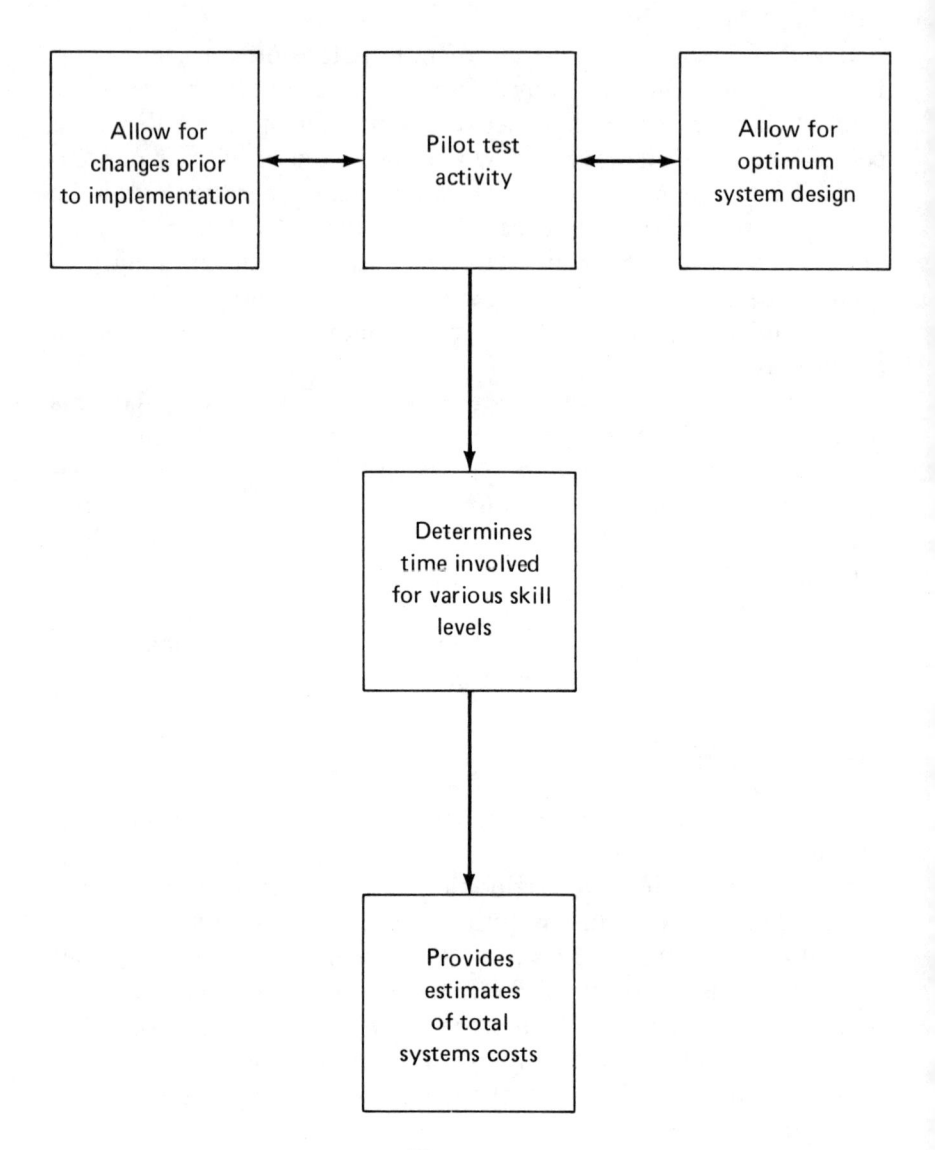

```
┌──────────────────┐      ┌──────────────┐      ┌──────────────────┐
│   Allow for      │      │              │      │   Allow for      │
│  changes prior   │◄────►│  Pilot test  │◄────►│    optimum       │
│ to implementation│      │   activity   │      │  system design   │
└──────────────────┘      └──────┬───────┘      └──────────────────┘
                                 │
                                 ▼
                        ┌──────────────┐
                        │  Determines  │
                        │ time involved│
                        │for various skill│
                        │    levels    │
                        └──────┬───────┘
                               │
                               ▼
                        ┌──────────────┐
                        │   Provides   │
                        │   estimates  │
                        │   of total   │
                        │ systems costs│
                        └──────────────┘
```

Figure 11-8

and concepts. As long as something is on the drawing board, we do not know how it will work. There may be a number of possibilities that are suggested and look good but what we do not know is whether or not they will work in actual practice. A pilot test situation gives us an opportunity to try these out. Those that prove themselves will be kept, and those that do not will be discarded.

A definite cost factor comes into play here. How many test sessions are enough? How many new ideas is it cost feasible to test? These are items that have to be decided on an individual basis. One pilot test is usually not enough, and normally, two or three seem to be the rule. The length and duration of these will vary from organization to organization. It generally takes a few months to fully check out most systems. Some people are satisfied with a shorter period of time if no major problems are encountered during the earlier stages.

The pilot test period also serves as a time for "fine tuning." This too is an area where costs can be incurred. An example might be in finding that a part of the instruction package is not as clear as it might be. This can present a very real cost related decision. To change the package would probably require changing the master. In many cases the master is on plates and so it can be a costly change. On the other hand, not making the change and leaving the instructions as they are, has a cost. If this portion is unclear, it will have an impact on the time it takes employees to complete, as well as allowing possibly inaccurate data to be collected as a result of it.

Some organizations avoid certain of the problems noted above by not piloting a final product. For example, the forms and instructions may be typed as rough copies. This definitely allows the piloting activity to take place at a reduced cost. Some feel that the pilot is not as accurate without using a more finished product. This is another area where the anticipated benefit to be derived has to be compared to the cost to be incurred. On the average, most firms tend to go with the rough typed material and then with the actual material for one last round of pilot testing. This method seems to satisfy everyone and ensures that the system is fully operational before going "live."

The pilot gives us another very important cost benchmark. This is the time it takes an employee to complete the process of filling out the skills inventory form. After a series of pilot tests we have a fairly good picture not only of the average time it will take, but the range of the time involved—when the fastest person will be finished, and when the slowest person will be finished. This may seem trivial, but if the form is to be completed, let us say, during a staff meeting, it is very important. Those coordinating need to be able to give supervision an estimate on how long a period to schedule the staff meeting for.

The time element is also important in determining the overall cost of the skills inventory to the organization. If we are having them completed during working hours, there are very large costs associated with the initial input. Then there is the time required during update phases. In addition, there will be the time of future new hires who will be completing the inventory as they enter the system.

Even where the instructions indicate that the form is to be completed at home or on the employees' own time, we know a percentage will not be completed. To be accurate this cost cannot be ignored. In addition, there is always the possibility that a union action may require that this home completion policy be avoided. For contingency planning this should always be considered as a possibility.

TIME REQUIRED TO BRING INVENTORY UP

There is an old adage that "if you are willing to spend enough money you can do anything". This certainly applies to the development of a skills inventory. It also has impact on the costs involved. Just how fast do we want the system up and running? How much are we willing to spend to meet these time frames?

Consider for instance that we are going to use internal capability to design and program the system. Cost can be affected directly by the time we determine the system must be ready by. If this is flexible, an arrangement may be made to use slack time between other projects to accomplish this. Costs would be miminized in this event.

On the other hand, assume that orders have gone out to get the system up and running right away. Top management has assigned a number one priority to it. This presents quite a different picture and quite a different cost impact. Other projects are put to the side.

These may be the ones that provide revenues or cost savings and are now themselves costs to our inventory. Additional staff with the related costs may have to be hired.

There is always the option of going to the vendor/consultant for assistance. If nothing else, we may want to go to a job shop to get programming assistance during critical periods. We can also add administrative help from agencies to beef up our support in the major distribution effort in the intitial data collection and distribution stages.

ACCURACY OF COST ESTIMATES

There is always the question of just how accurate the cost estimates are for any system. It is very much like building a house. Once you get started, all types of new ideas and opportunities seem to appear, and the building stage is the time to take advantage of these. You know that you are not going to get a chance to add the later, or if you do, it will be a major modification.

Those that have been involved in systems design realize that a reserve for contingencies is a definite requirement. How large should this contingency reserve be for an organization? The answer to this has to come from those involved, and to be based on their past experience. It may not be good practice to answer a question with a question, but this one seems an appropriate exception. How accurate have your past systems cost estimates been? If they have been consistently off by forty or fifty percent, there seems to be a benchmark established, and there is no reason to assume the skills inventory is going to be any different from the rest. Rather than delude yourself, apply the appropriate contingency factor, and then no one will be surprised by the final results.

Many organizations establish procedures to control potential cost overruns. One method that is frequently found is a review committee which is responsible for overseeing the project, and to whom any cost variances must be justified. This type of committee may or may not be effective. It does force those involved to focus more attention on the matter of costs, but many people debate the total overall effectiveness of this type of control. However, most agree that the higher the rank of those on the committee, the more apt it is to truly function as a controlling body. Most control committees that are staffed from lower echelons in the organization too often wind up as nothing but "rubber stamps." They continue to approve cost overruns because they lack the clout to do anything about them. This type of group usually does more damage than good, and wastes time that could be spent in more productive activities.

A cost control method that seems to have a positive impact utilizes some of the concepts of project management. Under this method of detailed description of tasks, the target completion dates are established, not while the project is operational, but before it is approved for implementation.

If properly done, this makes the planning phase long and detailed. Each task has to be identified from the beginning of the project to the end. This is probably the secret to the success of this method. Take a few minutes and think about prior systems or projects that exceeded cost projections. How many of them were due to "wild cards," or due to totally unforeseen events? How many could have been identified early? These probably turn out to be in the minority.

Listen to the planning that goes into setting up most projects, including skills inventories. Most often the time to complete a specific area is given in weeks, or usually in months. "We estimate it will take six weeks to design and test the turnaround document." Or "the instruction packages can be ready within two months from the time we are given the word to go."

These types of estimates are easy to give, and having to deliver is always safely in the future. The future has a way of rapidly becoming today. Now you hear things like, "say, we are going to need a few more weeks on that turnaround document, we had to pull some of our people for another project." Or "it looks like the instruction package won't be ready until after the third month, we found there was more involved than we estimated."

We have all known this to happen. What we are witnessing is the result of incomplete planning. When one part or more of the project slips, it has an impact on those further down the line. It is very likely that problems in the turnaround document and the instruction packages will slip the pilot tests. These may have to be cancelled and rearranged, which in turn has an impact on future phases. By the time we get to the end of the project the target date may be a month or more off base.

The costs involved are usually directly affected by target dates being missed. Frequently, enough man hours were not allocated. This in itself jumps the cost up, even if no other factors are involved. Also, a bottleneck at one stage of the project can throw us into costly overtime.

Now, let us get back to what can be done to avoid these costly and time consuming problems. Proper planning was identified as the key to this problem. The major tasks have to be identified, and the sub-tasks under them have to be spelled out in detail. For instance, we have been talking about the design of the turnaround document as one major task. There may be twenty or more items which go into this. There is the layout of the form, spacing for data entry, color coding, item sequences, etc. Should one of these fall behind schedule, it can have an impact on other areas, and later, very possibly on the timing of other major tasks.

The next step in ensuring costs are kept under control is to add a time factor to each major and each sub-task. Identify when the task starts and when completion is estimated. This is necessary both for the major tasks, and for each part of each task. This way there is an early warning system. If the color coding for the turnaround was to be accomplished by June first, and if it appears that this part of the project is off schedule, it is still early enough to do something about it.

Taking early action on time slippage is important. The secret to doing this is to set up an early warning system so you know when slippage is first starting, and take corrective action. It is too late when the project completion date has been reached, and you find out the entire system needs a least another three months.

MAKE OR BUY COSTS

At various times throughout this book we have discussed the make or buy considerations in skills inventory systems. Should we design our own system, get the assistance of a vendor/consultant, or use some combination? It is now time to look at these considerations in light of the cost factors involved. As in most decisions, these are usually the most significant factors in the entire decision making process.

We often make the mistake of thinking that we are spending money when we go outside the organization which we could save "by doing it ourselves." Many of us carry over our home improvement ideas into the business world. If we fix the leaky faucet over the weekend, then we save money by not having a plumber come to do the job.

Is it to be hoped that we do not have the systems analysts, programmers, and other personnel, sitting around with large chunks of idle time on their hands. When we perform a task using our own resources there is a very definite cost because this time could be spent on other projects. It is not free because we are doing it ourselves". The old adage "time is money" always applies.

The first thing we need to identify is what it will cost to design our own skills inventory system. In fact we should cost it out by each task involved. Then we can go to the vendor/consultants for their estimates. We are interested in possibly several different types of bids.

First we might be interested in what the charge will be for the entire project. Secondly, we may very well be interested in the cost for a part or parts of it. There may be areas in which we just do not have the required capability, and do not intend to try to hire or train for it. In this way we obtain more accurate cost considerations on which to base our decision.

MANAGEMENT GOALS

In this chapter we have spent a great deal of time looking at costs. This gives the impression that dollars are the only item in the equation. In some firms and under some managements this is very true. However, there are many cases where an organization wants something for reasons other than the cost/savings or monetary implications.

Managers and the organizations they represent have their pride and their psychological needs and requirements. Frequently the costs related to having a skills inventory system are not the paramount item of importance. Management may want an inventory for no other reason than that an associated organization has one. It is one more perquisite or status symbol that allows them to deal with their peers on an equal basis. Sometimes the frequently quoted "bottom line" gives way to some down-to-earth human psychology.

12
MAXIMUM USE OF THE SYSTEM

WHEN TO USE THE SYSTEM

The solution to the problem of when to use the system is largely controlled by the system's design. The first question that needs to be answered is whether or not the skills inventory is directly tied to the requisition system. In other words is every requisition tested against the skills inventory system before other recruiting and hiring efforts are made?

We discussed this earlier and stated that tying the inventory system to all open jobs is a significant goal. Supervisors and the employees alike know that at least one major internal source for candidates was reviewed before going further. This has a very positive effect on everyone using the system. Employees always feel certain that most of the information they are required to fill out is a waste of time. If it is not used, this assumption is one hundred percent correct. It does not take long for the word to spread that every job opening is passed against the inventory system. Those that are interested in advancement and promotion will want to insure their data is accurate and up-to-date.

INVENTORIES NOT TIED TO REQUISITION SYSTEM

Probably the largest portion of skills inventories are not tied to requisition systems. These are systems that have search capability, but usually leave up to the supervisor, or in some cases to an employment representative the decision whether to use the system in a given instance.

Some organizations establish policies on the use of such systems. Search requests may be required to be made on all salaried jobs above a certain level, or between certain rate ranges. Others may require that all openings in certain job categories or classifications be searched. This still places a certain amount of responsibility on management or supervisors to make a determination of which jobs will be tested against the system. In many cases, it is just left up to supervisors whether or not to use the skills inventory. It is not as all inclusive as our previous situation where all open requisitions were first checked against the system.

Here we are using a system in a somewhat unstructured environment. With the choices of using the system lying to a large extent with management, they will need some guidelines for making search requests. Possibly a form similar to the one shown in Figure 12.1 would be of assistance. It is simple and provides some of the basic information that most supervisors can readily provide. It is not so complete that detailed instructions are required to support it.

Some organizations develop more complex request forms for making job opening searches. There are two schools of thought on the subject: One feels that it speeds up the process and insures much higher accuracy of the searches; the other feels that it tends to make the process more complex and discourages supervision from using the system. Normally when there are two schools of thought, there is something to be said for both.

NEED FOR A RESIDENT SEARCH EXPERT

A very real problem is becoming apparent in these discussions. There is a need for a skills inventory search expert or experts to be available to assist supervisors with questions, and guide them in exploring their search needs and problems. Forms such as the one developed in Figure 12.1 can serve as an aid or a guideline.

The previous discussion dealt with requests for searches related to hiring. There are other types of searches that are going to occur. These might include language capability to assist in translating a document, a survey on degrees or majors, lists of professional organizations, etc. Too often we think of the inventory in its basic

INVENTORY SEARCH REQUEST

Requesting supervisor: _____

Department name: _____

Telephone number: _____

Organization code: _____

Mail code: _____

Briefly describe the position to be filled. Try to use key words in the description from the Skills Inventory Booklet when appropriate. Attach a job description if available.

Position Summary: _____

_____

_____

_____

_____

_____

Requesting Signature: _____ Date: _____

Figure 12-1

sense of use, which is to provide lists of candidates for job openings. This is a major function of any skills inventory, but certainly not the only one.

After we get away from the basic concept of identifying candidates for job openings, the inventory expert is needed to an even greater extent. When dealing with job openings there are a limited number of parameters that go into setting up a search. To a large extent, the system is designed around this search principle.

It is in searches in other areas where there is little past precedent or experience that true creativity is required. Supervisors soon learn what the system can do for the hiring activity. In other areas, such as those listing people desiring a location change or job preference move, assistance or intervention may be needed. Management will also require guidance in using the system for survey purposes.

Further down the line, there will be questions regarding merging information on the skills inventory file with other files that may be in existence. Here again, an expert on the system truly comes in handy. There are always cases when certain information on the inventory could be even more useful if combined with data elements from another file. For instance, let us take for a hypothetical example of a special tax survey that is being conducted. The survey may need to determine the average taxes withheld for masters degrees versus bachelors or the non-degreed segment. Part of the information is carried on the skills inventory file (degree data) and part on the payroll file (taxes withheld). This is a mini example of the type of situation that can and will arise. In actual practice, the requests are usually more complex, requiring in-depth knowledge of both systems in order to properly produce and evaluate the required output.

Structured forms are nice, but they cannot answer questions and explore alternatives. One of the questions that comes up is how much time must be dedicated to performing this function? This will vary from organization to organization. It will depend on the size of the file and the use that is made of it. In most medium-sized firms this becomes an additional duty for someone with a fairly good understanding of both personnel and systems. In major organizations of ten thousand or more employees, there may be several people dedicated to this task on a full time basis.

Where a vendor/consultant is involved some firms are contracting out this task. They do not want the addition to their own workload and would rather have it done for them. They may assign a focal point in their organization both to insure internal security, and to insure that the information requests are reasonable and justified. Beyond that, the search request or problem is turned over to the vendor/consultant for response. A diagram of this activity is shown in Figure 12.2.

OPTIMUM INVENTORY

Many firms have considerable difficulty in determining what the optimum skills inventory will be. How many categories should they have, what should or should not be included? The concern focuses on response time, will it be immediate, one day, a week? Too often these decisions are made by the analysts or the project head in charge of setting up the skills inventory system.

Many fail to make use of the very valuable resource available to them for review and input to the system. This is the existing team of managers and supervisors present in any organization. Too often the skills inventory is presented to them only after it has been finalized, or is in the final phases of completion. At this stage most people hesitate to make comments or suggestions. It is like your neighbor asking what you think of his new car when he drives it home from the sales room. If you were asked ahead of time which of the cars on the market you felt were good and why, your answer would probably be quite a bit different.

A good time to get management's input is in the very beginning. Bench mark off an existing inventory system others are using, pass it around and indicate that there is consideration being given to starting a similar system. Ask for comments, suggestions, modifications and let them know this is someone else's system, and that ideas are being solicited for the one to be used in their organization. Several drafts will be made in the process of developing the proposed system. Make sure these are passed around and the comments acted upon. Support for the final skills inventory will be much more

Maximum Use of the System 173

SEARCH ACTIVITY
CONDUCTED OUTSIDE

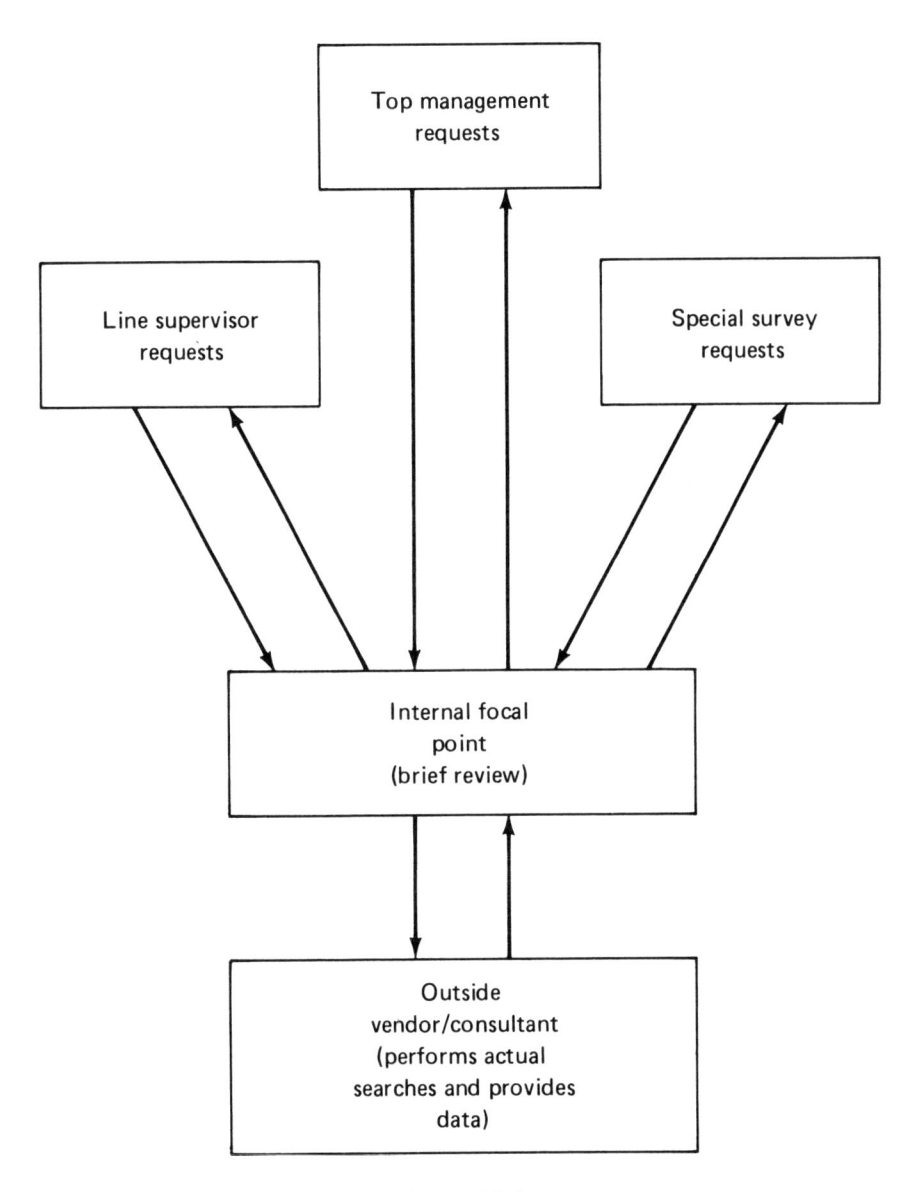

```
                    ┌──────────────┐
                    │Top management│
                    │   requests   │
                    └──────────────┘

┌──────────────┐                      ┌──────────────┐
│Line supervisor│                     │Special survey│
│   requests   │                      │   requests   │
└──────────────┘                      └──────────────┘

              ┌────────────────────┐
              │   Internal focal   │
              │       point        │
              │   (brief review)   │
              └────────────────────┘

              ┌────────────────────┐
              │      Outside       │
              │ vendor/consultant  │
              │  (performs actual  │
              │ searches and provides│
              │        data)       │
              └────────────────────┘
```

Figure 12-1

positive, since everyone has had an opportunity to be involved. It is "their" system and not "that" system.

The same thing applies to a vendor/consultant system. Supposedly you will be reviewing several possible proposals. These should be thoroughly circulated and comments solicited. It may take some additional time, but the end product is worth it. You will have a system that is better tailored to your organization, plus the support of those who will be using it. Remember, the users can see to it that even the best system does not work and without their support you have nothing.

INTRODUCING THE SYSTEM

Properly presenting the system to the employees is very important. Most people resist anything new and hate to fill out additional paper. One initial reaction will deal with the fact that most of the information has been given to management before in job applications, etc. Just entering an organization requires the completion of reams of data. Now the organization wants them to complete more paper, and is requesting some of the same information previously provided.

The best way is to confront this head on. Explain that you know you are asking for some of the same information again. The fastest way to get the information is with the employees' assistance and cooperation. It would take years of clerical time to dig through the personnel folders and other files to get the data. Even then, a lot of it would be out of date.

At the same time, if there are sufficient automated files so that some of the data can be pre-printed on the form for the employee it might be worth considering. Suppose an elaborate degree, college, major file had previously been established. You might be able to read this back onto the individual employee forms during the initial completion phase. If this proves impractical for any number of reasons, be certain this is explained to the employee. Most people are cooperative if they know why. Take the time to explain, and numerous problems can be avoided.

PRIVACY ISSUE

This is another area that you must not "sweep under the rug." Skills inventory data takes on some very personal and private aspects to many people. Privacy legislation of varying forms is in the news almost every day. It has significant implications to both managers and employees.

One solution may be to make the skills inventory voluntary. Only those who wish to participate are asked to complete the forms. Those who are concerned about what will or might happen to the data will not have to be involved.

This, of course, will cause a lower participation rate and will negate or reduce the value of the inventory for certain survey uses. It causes management to enter into more of a selling campaign, stressing the benefits of potential promotion, not being lost in the system, higher individual visibility, etc. This will very seldom, if ever, achieve the same system participation as a mandatory completion requirement.

What if the decision is made that a mandatory system is desired? What steps should management take to insure that it is acting within proper legal bounds? As we know legislation in the privacy area, as in most areas of personnel, is changing and evolving. Decisions in this area should be periodically reviewed by legal counsel. Most large organizations already employ in-house staffs for this purpose. Those that are not large enough to do so have usually established an outside firm on a retainer basis.

USE OF FORMAL ANNOUNCEMENTS

The first step has been the bringing of all levels of management on board regarding the use of a new skills inventory system. As with any management tool this should be a tops down briefing. Any system will work better, be implemented more smoothly, and overcome the initial obstacles much easier if it has top level support.

Each organization has its own political climate and taboos, but very few people get into serious trouble by asking for the president's or chairman's support on kicking off a new program. On the contrary, most are anxious to support and encourage these new programs. Go to the very top and ask for both support and endorsement. Chances are very good that it will not only be there, but will be there with the strong, enthustiastic support which is needed.

If the firm is large and/or geographically spread out, you may wish to employ some of the media techniques for getting the word out. Why not a film with the president of the company introducing the skills inventory? This is much more intimate than a letter, and can be put together rather rapidly with today's film technology. If the organization does not possess its own, there are many independent producers who specialize in the industrial market.

Film may not be feasible from an economic point of view. It may not be the type of item your organization can handle in its budget. What about a brochure, with a few colored pictures and an informal statement written by the president? "This is a new system and we want to emphasize management's support." Something different is needed. Try to use some thing that is outside the normal communication media. Many firms involved in graphic arts and related products can come up with alternate concepts, ideas that you may have thought of, and ones that are well within your budget.

We talked about getting management and supervisors involved and briefed on the system. In addition, they need to be supplied with a consistent set of tools to carry out their function of informing their staff. If there is to be a film or other material, they should be provided with sufficient copies to get the job done. It is better if all briefings can take place as close together as possible. This way questions and responsible answers can come through supervisors rather than from informal, and sometimes uninformed sources.

Do not assume that supervisors know what you want presented. It is easier all the way around if they are provided with a staff meeting guideline. Those who developed the inventory were probably also active in its pilot test. They have some idea of the questions that employees normally have regarding the system. These should be listed along with the corresponding possible answers. This type of preparation allows supervision to come across in a knowledgeable and professional way. It shows that the system and related problems have been thought out and provided for.

Some firms are small enough for the person responsible for the skills inventory to make the rounds and give the presentations. This can be a plus or a minus depending on the factors involved. Answering questions and providing details on the system can be handled much more easily and accurately by the expert. Yet there is sometimes something lost in not having the people hear it from their own manager or supervisor, even though the expert is better at presenting the system. When they know the boss is presenting the system and is fully behind it, it carries more weight than when the presentation is made by someone from an outside area.

USING THE HOUSE ORGAN

A number of firms of the size and complexity to have an operational skills inventory also have their own internal publication, newspaper or newsletter. This is commonly referred to as the "house organ," it is a good place to present the inventory to the staff from several points of view.

It can be especially effective if the publication is held in high regard. House organs are no different than any other communications channel. There are those which are viewed as being reliable and excellent information sources, and some of questionable value. We want to use the house organ as a vehicle for information regarding the skills inventory only if it has a positive organizational image. Should it have a poor image, its use can do more damage than good.

The question arises as to how one tells if the image is good or not. The publisher and staff are usually going to be favorable regardless. Management may or may not know, depending on how attuned they are to items of this nature. It is doubtful that the house organ is high on their list of concerns. If an active research group exists, an employee attitude survey may have been made. This is at least worth asking for in the event a current one is not available.

Aside from using these methods we can always do a bit of

checking indirectly. Most people will readily complain if something displeases them. Raise the topic over coffee. What type of response is received? Ask a few questions about past articles or announcements. First, did anyone even remember them? If not that tells us something about the overall esteem in which it is held. If they did read them, what was the reaction, positive, negative or not written clearly enough for anyone to have an opinion? This may not be the most scientific approach to determining how the house organ is viewed, yet it often gives us sufficient insight. Negative feelings strong enough to do damage to the inventory, if we use this media, can probably be identified in time.

Assuming that the house organ checks out and is rated as satisfactory, there are several possible applications. First it can be used in making the initial announcement, possibly even months in advance of the actual implementation. A series of articles can be a good way to let the employees know the organization is planning such a system. Their comments and suggestions can be solicited at this point, and implemented when appropriate.

Then it can serve as a vehicle to go along with the film or other major announcement at the time of full implementation. It should not be used as the only vehicle, but as an adjunct. It is a good place to stress the positive aspects of the system. A skills inventory can be a true benefit to those interested in eliciting strong responses and support.

The house organ can also serve as a follow-on support item after the system is up and in progress. Remember, management usually has insight as to how the system is progressing, but what about the employees? They have put forth a certain amount of effort to complete the forms and provide input into the system. Those interested in promotion and upward mobility are usually the same people that have a need for information and status reports.

We all like feedback on our efforts. If we have put something into the system, we expect something out of the system. The house organ can serve as a way of keeping the people informed of where the system is and where it is going. The number of participants and state of the data base will be of interest. It may help to increase participation. Suppose only fifty percent of the people are participating in the system. It can honestly be stressed that the odds of being considered are greater than if everyone were in the system.

FALSE EXPECTATIONS

One thing we need to guard against is the creation of false expectations about participation in the skills inventory system. This statement may almost seem at odds with what has been discussed, but it must be emphasized. In all our efforts to gain support and participation in the system, its limits must also be pointed out.

The house organ may be a fair way to explore this aspect. The skills inventory may increase the odds of being identified as a candidate. It is another tool to aid management in identifying candidates. It does not guarantee that everyone who is in the system will get a new job, promotion, higher salary, or whatever the case may be.

Though this is in a negative vein, management would be very wise to impress this upon those involved. Rather than discouraging people from participating in the system, candor will probably bring added support. Many of the employees will already realize the odds involved. Most of them can deal with accurate facts, but want no part of false hopes and promises. We want to be honest and stress the positive facts about skills inventories fairly, and we must be just as honest about the negative aspects.

EMPHASIZING THE POSITIVE

Searches are going to result in candidate lists being produced. There will be selections made from these lists which are the direct result of the skills inventory. Here, every effort should be made to publicize this fact. Again, the house organ can be a very useful tool in doing this.

By the same token, we want to respect the privacy of the individuals who may have been selected as a result of the search. Prior to any publicity, the employees involved should be contacted, so that their permission for publicity may be obtained. We want the system to work for the employees and we want their respect and confidence.

This means consulting them on items that could directly affect their personal privacy. In reality, you will find most people are more than willing to participate and will enjoy being in the limelight.

Many more people appear on candidate lists than are ever selected for a position. This is an honest assessment, and one that has a very sizeable psychological impact. For instance, assume that an organization employs twenty thousand people, and over five thousand appeared on various skills inventory searches throughout the year. That number probably has more impact than the actual selection figures. Most people are interested in insuring that they will be considered, if at all eligible. These types of numbers will never satisfy everyone, but they do lend a good deal of credence to the organization's efforts to insure that qualified candidates are not overlooked.

13
WHY INVENTORIES HAVE FAILED

INVENTORY FAILURES

The word failure has a definite negative connotation. Failure can also be a learning experience, in that we know what not to do next time. Proper attention to this aspect can provide additional guidelines which success models do not point out. Failure can and should be a learning experience.

What we want to avoid is the trial-and-error method. If possible we want to learn by mistakes that have already been made. In essence let us see if we cannot learn from the failure of others, rather than by pioneering in the area ourselves.

We normally observe two types of failures with skills inventories. The first one is the most obvious. The system has not met management needs and the determination has been made to scrap it. In some cases effort is immediately started to get another system. In others, management just writes the entire concept off as a bad venture.

Proportionately, there are not too many of these types of failure. Very few organizations give up on the concept completely. It seems to have too many desirable elements to write it off completely. More often than not, you will find organizations going on to second and third efforts until they find one which works.

One firm went through this process several times. Their first system collapsed miserably. Follow-up efforts met with a little more success, but were ultimately canceled. They learned from these experiences and continued their development efforts. A system was

182 Planning and Using Skills Inventory Systems

finally developed that met their management's needs and became an industry model. In fact, the system was so successful that the firm has been marketing it to other organizations for several years. It has a reputation for being one of the best skills inventories around.

The second type of skills inventory failure may be harder to detect. This is the one where the system exists almost in name only. It is physically there, but hardly ever used. Some of those reading this may have such a system. It is probably the most costly type of skills inventory. In most cases the maintenance activity continues, with programs being maintained, forms stocked, periodic updates conducted, etc. The expense or overhead time continue, but there is not sufficient use to offset any of these expenses.

Skills inventories are not the only types of systems that have died with no one really knowing it. Why does this occur? In some cases management may just want the status symbol of being able to say they have "such and such type of system." In other cases they do not realize that it is not being used. Possibly no one is assigned formal responsibility for monitoring the usage and productivity. It may be that no one knows what the system should have achieved in the first place.

There are several potential solutions to identifying and solving this type of problem. Several times earlier we have discussed a type of "ideal" system where the skills inventory is tied to the requisition and hiring system. In this case, activity logs of searches should be maintained and periodic reports requested by management. They should be checking closely on the usage and time intervals between search requests.

If all else fails, there is the old-fashioned method of testing any system. Continue to produce the products, but do not distribute them; wait and see who, if anyone, complains. Do not send out biographies, listings, updates, etc. Temporarily discontinue searches, or wait until the second request. This type of test should be conducted with management knowledge, so the unit does not appear to be slacking off or unresponsive.

It should not take too long before we find out how important or unimportant our skills inventory is. People tend to follow up something that is useful or has importance to them. Payroll checks need only be a few hours late before phones are ringing off the hook. We cannot expect this type of response for the skills inventory, but if no one notices it is missing after a month or two you can give odds that it is in real trouble.

PROBLEM FACTORS

There is a thread of consistent factors that seem to appear in every inventory system that gets into trouble. We will discuss the major ones that have been noted through actual field experience. One or more factors seem to be enough to seriously impact on the skills inventory. In most cases, these are severe enough to throw the system into serious trouble.

Sheer size and bulk of the skills inventory has always been a major factor. This is particularly addressed to the instruction package. Some of these have been produced that almost appear to be small phone books. Employees are shocked at the thought of having to go through something of this magnitude in order to identify themselves.

Too often, the designer of the instruction package wants to make certain that everything has been included and nothing overlooked. True success in this area often dooms the system to failure. Employees either refuse to fill out the form using this as a guideline, or flip through it in a hurry because they want to get finished. The entire attempt by the designer resulted in overkill.

What is the appropriate size or length? You can get arguments on this all day and all night. The best way is to look at systems that are successful and have been operating for several years. Most seem to limit their instruction packages, including the word lists, to fewer than fifty pages, and the input form to one or two pages. Within reason, the less overwhelming the instruction packages and word lists, the more successful the system. There are exceptions to this, but generally speaking small is beautiful and more frequently successful.

If you are going to produce large quantities of papers and lengthy lists, it takes a certain type of organization to stand for it. You can do this in a military environment where you can issue orders regarding its use and demand compliance. In the private sector, particularly with highly mobile (in demand) skills and positions, you must be very careful. These people possess a high degree of autonomy, and a very low tolerance for paperwork. You are apt to wind up with more problems than just negative responses or lack of participation.

There are ways to get the information across and keep the paper volume down. One technique that effective systems tend to use is pictures, diagrams, and examples, rather than text. The old saying "a picture is worth a thousand words," certainly applies. Not only does it reduce the bulk, but if properly done makes the instructions much more understandable. The text can be photo-reduced. If professionally done, this can reduce many pages to a few. Again, this must be handled in such a way as to achieve proper proportion. Too much reduction, and we create an eyestrain situation.

OVER-ENGINEERING THE SYSTEM

Many systems are over-engineered, which constitutes another problem. The instructions are complex, and the forms are too detailed. Information is requested that is never used and that does not serve any purpose.

Often these forms and instructions are designed by people with a heavy data processing background. This is logical, because the systems are often run on computer systems, and require technical assistance and guidance. Frequently, the focus is on the technical design of the form and the instructions, rather than on the human aspect. Somewhere we have to achieve a blend of the efforts involved. The system has to be designed to accommodate the technical portion—we have to enter the data satisfactorily into any automated system. At the same time, we are getting the data from people, and have to allow for their specific needs and problems. Without them, there is no data at all.

The forms and instructions must be designed for the average person, and not the data-entry professional. One way to attempt to assure this is to have good representation on the design group. This should include people from non-technical areas. In the initial pilot phase, pay particular attention to this aspect.

Some organizations develop a pilot questionnaire and this is one of the items noted (See Figure 13.1). This is a good way to see if the

PILOT QUESTIONNAIRE

1. Did you find the instruction package adequate?

    Yes ☐   No ☐

    If no, please explain: _____

    _____

2. Did you find the form adequate?   Yes ☐   No ☐

    If no, please explain: _____

    _____

3. Are there any modifications you would like to see made?

    Yes ☐   No ☐

    If yes, please explain: _____

    _____

4. Any other items you wish to comment on: _____

    _____

    _____

Figure 13-1

system has been over-engineered. Some of the key questions should be aimed at the form and the instruction manual. This is the time to "smoke out" and identify problem areas. It is much easier to correct them at this point, before the system goes throughout the organization.

DESIGNED FOR SAMPLE WORKFORCE SEGMENT

Often the skills inventory has been designed primarily for a professional segment of the work force. For instance, if the idea and original requirement for the system originated from engineering management, it would be normal that they head up the original study team and very heavily control the input and structure.

As the system expands, it must take into account other areas such as production control, manufacturing, personnel, etc. It is hoped that each of these areas will be contacted and have an input. A problem that may arise is the professional tone of the inventory and the areas with which it is coordinated. Remember, the guiding force has been a very professional and technical part of the organization. Those responding from other areas tend to sense this tone and then respond in a similar way.

This type of response is a concern if we really plan on expanding the inventory into all areas of the organization. Do we want to use it for hourly as well as salaried employees? Is the aim now or in the future to include non-professionals as well as professionals? Should either of these be the case, then we may be structuring the inventory wrongly to begin with. By providing word structures that cover everyone, we preclude programming ourselves for further problems and possible failure of the system.

TOO BROAD A COVERAGE

Some inventories try to cover every possible industry, firm, organization, etc., in one package. This is a very difficult task, and may not be possible. There are some all-purpose systems that are purportedly able to handle any organization. However, those systems are the ones that often need to be tailored to an individual operation.

One of the problems that employees encounter in a non-tailored system is the volume of unrelated material they must go through to identify themselves. Usually, it is easier and faster if the word system is directly related to the organization involved. Many systems designers are recognizing this as a potential problem, and are setting up separate packages by specific industry and/or tailoring a system for each individual organization.

KEY WORD DICTIONARY AND TOTAL WORD PACKAGE

As we discussed earlier, this is the heart of the system. It can also be the part of the inventory that contributes significantly to the success or failure of the system. A well-designed key word system will go a long way toward keeping the system operational, even if some of the other negative factors are present.

It should be designed to deal with terms and descriptive words familiar and used in everyday operation within the organization. Those lists fully circulated and approved by the firm's management prior to implementation seem to have the most success. Key word systems which are not coordinated, and which management is either not familiar or comfortable with are potential trouble spots.

Going a step further, the successful packages have usually been fully coordinated and approved by management. This concept may seem repetitious, but it is so important to the smooth operation of the skills inventory. Each management has a set of terms or jargon that it is comfortable with. Provide them with this in a format that fits into the organization picture, and you automatically have a certain amount of success and acceptance. Ignore it, and that managememt feels it is dealing with something foreign and uncomfortable. Being human, most people tend to shy away from situations in this category. This is the opposite of the behavior we are trying to cultivate.

COSTS AND JUSTIFICATION

An earlier chapter was devoted to the costs of keeping and running an inventory system. Unless you are marketing your system to others, it is going to represent an expense item. All expense items are constantly up for scrutiny as potential savings items.

Many of the benefits of a skills inventory system fall into the intangible category. When someone on staff is selected to fill an opening, this in turn creates another opening. Any savings in this type of situation are hard to identify. We know there is a value to a to these systems in all phases of the organization. The real problem is tying them to a specific dollar amount. When this cannot be done, it subjects a system to possible cancellation during periods of austerity. As all of us know, every organization goes through these periods on an almost predictable basis.

INVENTORIES USED DURING ECONOMIC UPSWINGS

This is a concept that is definitely tied to the success and failure of some systems. Truly outstanding skills inventories will continue during most types of economic activity. We do find systems that either fail or are temporarily shut down during times of economic slowdowns or recessions. These probably fall into the category of the marginally successful.

There are some very real management concerns that take place during economic upswings that tend to support this type of observation. First, there is a desire to maximize the skills available and training dollars spent. Heavy training is occurring as times get better, and fewer people are available on the market. Management wants to make certain they are getting a proper return on their investment. They see these dollars going out for training, and want to make certain people are placed properly and that full utilization of their skills is made.

Again, the skills inventory is seen as the vehicle to identify skills appropriately and assist in placing people. It is also viewed as a tool to identify people who need training. If you want everyone performing a specific function to have cost accounting in their background, a skills inventory search can identify both those that do and those that do not.

Identifying those who do not possess a given skill can be just as important as identifying those who do. The ones who do not possess it can constitute the pool of those who need to be put through a training program. In this manner we can assure ourselves that we have the skill mix we want by training on a selected basis. This avoids the "shotgun" approach and saves training dollars.

Also, during good economic times and when an organization is in a build-up phase you need good people. The business is there, and must be responded too or it will be lost to competition. Time is of the essence.

Management is interested in setting up inventories to aid in this time pressure crunch. They see these as instruments to assist in moving people into vital slots as fast as possible. Ideally, they would like to move people around in the middle and upper portions of the organization to fill any openings. These people already know the organization policies and procedures and do not require additional time to get up to speed.

Skills inventories are viewed as tools to aid in upward mobility. Theoretically, openings are filled internally by their use until we no longer have qualified candidates appearing. Under ideal conditions, management would like to see these types of movement continuing until the open slots are mostly entry level positions. In actual practice this full utilization of existing staff resources will never occur, but skills inventories are viewed as a vehicle in this goal.

Also, during build-up times it is a seller's market. The outside labor force is in demand, and it takes more work and recruitment dollars to attract good people. When other firms are competing for the same people prices are driven up. Management wants to fully use the people they already have, both because of the cost of recruiting in this market, and because of fear of losing their own valuable people. If they can provide upward mobility, they can meet their own requirements and possibly keep their people more satisfied.

The quality on the outside market is also an unknown quantity. It used to be that application forms could explore an applicant's background in great detail. Also, organizations were able rather freely to exchange background information regarding prior employees. This is no longer the case, and the law strongly limits exploration of applicants to the degree that used to exist.

These limitations make the recruiting and selection procedure more of a management concern than in the past. Moving present employees around is more favorable than going outside. You know what you have with a present employee. There is a work record, personnel folder, peer evaluation, and supervisor evaluations. With just a few phone calls you can fully check the backgrounds of your own employees without fear of lawsuits or other legal or government repercussions.

The same factor that makes a skills inventory valuable during a build-up phase is not as important during a downswing. When employees are readily available, sometimes to the point of excess, most firms are not as interested in inventories. Many inventories are canceled, or put on the shelf during this period.

Granted some of the products such as the biography may be reviewed in making a decision to layoff or retain someone, but not to the degree experienced during a build-up. Skills inventories may eventually take a stronger role in this area. With the human resource taking a role of more importance, these tools may further aid management in making staff reduction decisions. At present, their use in this area seems to be nominal.

14
MANPOWER PLANNING AND THE FUTURE

MANPOWER PLANNING OR STAFF PLANNING

The term manpower planning has been around for many years. It is a chauvinistic term that has had a recent name change. Usually you hear it referred to as staff planning, or human resource planning, to avoid the sexist inference which manpower planning might have.

The problem with these name changes is that often, no one is certain what you are talking about. It is like the various terms, personnel development, management development, that you hear used. You will hear these along with titles such as, manager of personnel development. A person not familiar with the organization will enter into a discussion to find out what type of work the person does. Ultimately one or the other will refer to training, or the training field, and communication will have been achieved. Our semantic games will probably be a source of humor to sociologists and social psychologists of the future.

One of the aims of this book is to achieve clear communications on the topic of skills inventories. Having to explain in conversation the meaning of staff planning, or human resource planning, indicates these and the other related terms are still not understood. For the sake of clarity and understanding the term manpower planning will be used. Those having difficulty or strong feelings about it, may feel free to mentally substitute their favorite non-sexist word. Remember that if it were possible to use some other word here and achieve full communication, it would be done.

WHY DEAL WITH THE MANPOWER PLANNING TOPIC?

We often hear the terms manpower planning and skills inventories used almost interchangeably. If you were to go to some organizations and asked about their manpower planning operation, they would show you their skills inventory system. There is a great deal of confusion between manpower planning and skills inventories.

The two are separate, and yet they are closely related. What we will do is explore the various aspects of manpower planning, and there are quite a few, and then we will tie this concept of manpower planning back into inventories and show how they interrelate.

CLASSICAL MANPOWER PLANNING

In some circles manpower planning is viewed almost as a crystal ball type of operation. This is where a group, through various means, informs management what the future will be like so far as staffing is concerned. Will we need four hundred more electrical engineers, fifty accountants, etc.? It is usually a field that is seen focusing heavily on the various techniques of forecasting and projecting.

One area that most organizations find to be a classic concern is the population mix. Particularly with the impact of the Affirmative Action laws this has been an area of attention. There is concern with the number of people by race and sex throughout all levels of the organization. Here we are concerned with both the present and the future. If there are inadequacies in the present, plans are made for corrective action in the future mix.

This concept is placed in the area of classical manpower planning concerns. The term classical tends to give a connotation of age or of having been in existence for a period of time. Possibly neoclassical would be a better term for population mix. In contrast to some of the other manpower planning concerns, it is relatively new. However, it is important at the present time, very probably will be in the near future, and will continue to be an item of attention.

The skills mix is truly a classical manpower planning item. This gets into the questions of how many of what type we need to perform the work. Next year will we need forty mechanical engineers or sixty? This type of knowledge can be critical for many related functions. Their own staffing and operation can be directly affected by changes of this magnitude.

For instance, if we go from twenty mechanical engineers to forty, this could have a very great impact on the personnel function. A lot will depend on market conditions and what type of recruiting problems are anticipated. Should there be large numbers of mechanical engineers available and looking for jobs, and if it is anticipated that this will continue, the problem is minor. However, if we anticipate a shortage of mechanical engineers on the labor market, the situation is entirely different.

In a shortage situation we know recruiting will be difficult. We may add to the recruiting staff to handle or consider using search firms to help us solve the problem. Regardless of which way we decide to go, we will be incurring significant costs. This may necessitate further management review and approval, since a budget overrun is most likely involved.

Additional staff usually requires more clerical support, and more office space, parking space, desks, chairs, etc. In an engineering or scientific environment there is often the need for lab or testing facilities along with the related support equipment.

Skills mix has another connotation other than the cost of adding or subtracting people. Often the work force is in a state of transition. The organization may be changing from a labor intensive clerical operation, to one that is converting to automation. The types of skills we use heavily today may not be the ones we will need tomorrow.

As rapid technological change is occurring, many organizations are confronted with this problem. What do you do with the existing staff? There are many options such as layoffs, early retirement, out placement assistance, etc. There is also the training or re-training that must take place for those who are going to be retained. Problems in this area are rapidly increasing. Organizations are becoming aware that there is a very human or social commitment to their staff. This is creating a compounded problem in the area of manpower planning.

Another classical, and sometimes critical problem in manpower planning, is retirement forecasting. This involves planning a smooth transfer as those eligible for retirement phase out and their replacements take over. Problems arise here because the ground rules for retirement do not always remain constant.

One example occurred in an engineering firm. Union negotiations reduced the age at which employees were eligible for retirement from sixty-five to fifty-five. It had been the company's policy to extend any new union benefits to all employees including those in administrative and management areas, and this meant the new retirement option applied to everyone.

A quick look at the firm's history showed it had grown from a basic manufacturing firm into a more sophisticated engineering operation. Those older employees had, in most instances, continued in the manufacturing departments. The younger new hires had moved into the engineering and scientific areas.

A very real problem had developed. The new retirement policy applied to almost the entire manufacturing group. In effect the entire manufacturing function throughout the firm would be wiped out if everyone elected to use his/her retirement options.

There are other areas that impact on this retirement picture other than changes in an organization's policy. Central to this are the various decisions created through state and federal legislation. Due to the high birth rate after World War II, there is a very large segment of the population in a specific age range. This "war baby boom" group is chugging through the system. It will create havoc if everyone in this group retires at the same time.

There is very little doubt that present retirement policies and laws will be changed to avoid this problem. Possibly under the guise of Affirmative Action, mandatory retirement will be significantly changed. Without this, the already shaky Social Security system will experience even greater difficulties.

Another classical manpower planning tool is the firm model. This has been made popular by the advances in computer technology. In very simple terms the concept is to put the organization's operations on a computer. Then you can change the variables to observe what impact this will have on the other variables. What will staff be if sales increase by twenty percent? What will happen to the stock of raw material if production is reduced by one half? This type of simulation allows you to observe what may happen without experiencing the actual occurence.

Modeling is still in its infancy. Problems always arise where we are trying to deal with major variables that have not been predicted. The oil crisis precipitated all kinds of problems with many models. Inflation rates and material costs skyrocketed out of sight. As long as these types of situations occur, there will always be a certain reluctance to more fully commit to the use of concept models.

ACTUAL PRACTICE

In the earlier description of classical systems we touched on only a few of them. There are others, but the significant factor is that this area of manpower planning exists. It is very important, for as can be seen, the problems involved are very real.

This type of classical data may provide management with some insight, but their reliance on it is still questionable. Most managers are flexible in staff control. They do not rely on crystal ball type projections.

More often than not, we wait until the crisis is present and then take action. Staff is controlled. It is usually allowed to grow during good times and favorable profits. Then it is cut when a recessionary period or a business downturn occurs. There may be some that say we have a higher degree of staff control than this.

If staff control is more sophisticated it is doubtful that we would experience the major layoffs which too frequently occur. Also, during the upswing there might not be the heavy use of overtime, long hours, weekends, etc. How often have you heard the statement, "it is either feast or famine"? The more classical tools are toyed with, but not truly implemented to smooth out all bumps.

Many organizations are being pressured into some new practices as they deal with the staffing problem. The staff commitment is becoming more of a permanent consideration. Major layoffs still occur, but create a public relations problem which did not previously exist.

Rather than making a staff commitment they are maintaining a central or cadre staff and purchasing other services. All types of agency and part-time arrangements are being made. These people are rented from agencies or put on the payroll on a temporary basis. This eases any future reduction that may have to occur due to economic or other considerations.

The same thing is occurring with the use of consultants. Rather than going outside and hiring someone to perform a function we purchase a consultant's services. The task is often accomplished much faster because of the experience involved. At the same time, there is no staff commitment past the end of the project contracted for.

MANPOWER PLANNER CAN PROVIDE TOOLS

We have looked at some of the classical practices and some of the actual concerns. The questions now are, what can the manpower planner do to aid management, and where does the skills inventory fit into this package?

In most cases management is looking for aids in decision making. It is suggested here that a flexible package of tools is desired, rather than crystal ball type activities. This is not to say that interest does not exist in projections and forecasts. These have not always met with the success that is desired, and consequently are not used to the degree many believe.

It does not take too many unexpected variables and missed targets before management loses faith. Projects and forecasts may be the ideal in the area of manpower planning, but let us keep them in proper perspective. They will be one of the functions in this area, but not the only one. There are many other tools that can provide management assistance with greater reliability and accuracy.

Manpower planners can engage in surveys of patterns of changing mix. Most department heads are sources for areas and items occurring in their areas. Also, most organizations are more freely exchanging such data. These efforts can be tied back to the classical mix studies, or projected into what we might call here the neoclassical mix studies, or projected into what we might call here the neoclassical activities.

Under the neoclassical we might explore the aspects of women in the labor force—creation of daycare centers, and possibly the changing patterns in child bearing age and family size. These items have an impact not only on our present labor pool, but on items such as the benefit package, part-time pool, etc.

Analysis of the changes in technology also has an impact on the mix, some of these have been determined and are scheduled or tentatively scheduled for implementation. Most of the cost studies and vendor analyses give us a picture of what impact these people have. The basic specifications spell out the savings by employing these new systems, and sometimes the requirements for the new people needed to operate these.

Another area in which the manpower planner can perform a valuable service is in determining training needs. This includes not only future training, but that which is needed here and now. Often everyone agrees that training is required, but "what and how much" is frequently the question that is not answered.

When we avoid the "what and how much" we tend to paint ourselves into a corner. Without actual identifiable needs, only pet projects sometimes of questionable value tend to occur. The manpower planning activity can provide valuable service in developing some needed tools. One of the first steps might be to develop measurements of length of time to bring someone up to speed in a given job.

There are some functions where trainees may be in the "pipeline" for several years before they are prepared to take over a complete function. Knowing this, plus knowing the turnover, and other factors, can give us an idea of how many must be in the system to achieve a given number in the multiple year time frame. In fact, for some organizations, just identifying that there is a time frame is a valuable service. This in essence forces the planning function to occur. Frequently, planning does not come about, and most of the efforts are directed at solving problems which are the direct result of its lack. This falls into the category of "fire fighting." These unplanned emergencies can take up tremendous amounts of an organization's time, resources, and overall energy.

In the training area there are very valid requirements for surveys based on both the type and quality of training. Training dollars spent today are the basis for production of the future. Properly providing management with systematic tools to identify training needs, and then going back with a set of tools to audit the quality, is an invaluable service.

Another area of concern that manpower planning can establish itself in is the area of internal placement. This covers the entire range of matching people and jobs. Here we could establish a transfer activity which aids people who are interested in another assignment or a higher level position. It also might be a supervisor's initiated transfer request to place an employee in a better position, or into one which offers more advancement than the supervisor views in his/her existing operation.

There is also the possibility of setting up a job posting system to allow employees more opportunity to know about jobs which open up. Here open requisitions are posted in the employee lounge or other convenient area for review by all those interested. In essence employees get the first opportunity to interview for a position before it goes to the outside for possible hiring.

These are just a few of the tools that the manpower planning group may institute. This list that we have discussed here is not all inclusive in any sense, nor was it intended to be. Each manpower planning group will have special tools which it can supply that will uniquely fit the needs of the management group which it serves.

WHERE DOES THE SKILLS INVENTORY FIT?

The skills inventory is one of the tools that is available to those involved in manpower planning. It is practical in nature and avoids the crystal ball approach, to which management frequently is not too responsive.

The skills inventory may be able to help, or be an adjunct to some of the other tools listed. There can be a definite use in the survey area as well as aiding in the establishment of the training pool. It also in an ideal system to provide candidate lists to assist in internal placement.

The skills inventory is one of the tools in manpower planning, and can be a significant aid or assist in applying some of the others. It is sometimes billed as being an entire manpower planning system by itself. Though it is a very powerful tool in this area, it is hard to conceive of it as being the entire manpower planning system. If no manpower planning system exists, a skills inventory may be a starting point or a building block. It can be an initial system to open the door in this area, with other systems or manpower planning tools following to aid in meeting an organization's requirements.

TODAY IS THE BASIS FOR THE FUTURE

There are certain things about the future of skills inventories that can be predicted. This does not require any special insight or extrasensory perception. All we have to do is to look at what is happening today. It has been said, and rightly so, that what we do today creates tomorrow's future. There may be new technology or other occurrences that produce major changes. However, in most cases the effort being made and the work being done at this time, lays the groundwork for what tomorrow will bring.

To a certain degree, it is like building a house or any other structure. The land is selected and the foundation that is laid will determine where, and of what type the structure will be. We have some very special solid foundations established in skills inventory areas. By reviewing these we can get a picture of some of the things to expect in the years to come.

EXPANDING USE

Most organizations desire the benefits of a skills inventory system. The market place has not ignored this, nor is it going to do so. The vendor/consultants that we discussed earlier are very sensitive to this, and have continued to expand the packages and services offered.

Personnel packages that could be installed to produce standard information reporting have been around for many years. These provide all types of related data, such as compensation reports, hiring statistics, affirmative action reports, and other relevant material. These are what we have been referring to here as "packaged systems."

Many of these systems have established good reputations. In addition, there is some excellent marketing support being provided. Their success has created quite a bit of competition, which has caused further review and expansion of their services. Many have added or are in the process of adding a skills inventory as part of their package.

The market seems definitely to be expanding for these systems. As new firms determine that they will go to these package systems, skills inventories become part of the transaction. This alone will add to the number of inventories that will be used in the future.

EDUCATION AND COST

Skills inventories certainly are not the rarity they were ten or twenty years ago. Those organizations not having them do not have to look very far to find one. They are in use in industry, government, education, and other areas. With the large number of vendor/consultants samples and and demonstrations can be brought right to the door.

The literature used to be almost void of any discussion of the topic. In recent years, a number of major journals and other publications have come forth with various articles and discussions on the inventories. Many new textbooks refer to the subject and devote anywhere from one to several pages on the subject. This is particularly true of those books in the management or personnel field. This means that many of the college students entering business will have some formal exposure to the concept.

Putting this together, we have some picture, or at least, an awareness, of the subject of skills inventories. Today's management is informed because systems are being brought to their door, and tomorrow's managers will have the added advantage of contact through the formal education process as well. We can assume with a high degree of accuracy that skills inventories, at least as far as definition, will not be a question mark in the minds of future managers. In fact, many should feel quite comfortable in dealing with the subject, and this is a major change from the past.

Costs of these systems are a little harder to pin down with as much certainty. We do know that they have decreased in some of the automated areas. Some may take exception to this statement, but there is evidence to support this stand. Computers and their related systems are no longer accessible only to large conglomerates. Small organizations are now able to avail themselves of this service as well, and they are doing so.

In the future, it seems that the cost of having access to a skills inventory system will come within the range of most organizations. If for no other reason, the competition by vendor/consultants will probably force this. The organizations themselves have a basic need for this type of tool. In a competitive market this quickly can become an addition to a larger package that helps to sell the prospective customer. Those in the field will realize this and price accordingly.

AFFIRMATIVE ACTION REQUIREMENTS

The government has taken an active role over the years to erase discrimination and related activities. There are laws, contractual sanctions, enforcement bodies, etc. involved in this activity. Almost any organization dealing with the government in any way is subject to involvement in support of this effort. The support required is not just verbal but of the active type.

Compliance officers periodically visit firms to follow up on their activities, and insure that discriminatory practices are not in effect. This is having a direct impact on skills inventories from two points of view. First, these compliance investigations require that the organization under review keep records and statistics. Secondly, many of these reviews indicate that a skills inventory system would be a positive additive to aid in avoiding discrimination during the internal selection process.

To improve their overall record keeping, organizations either design their own system, procure an outside system, or some combination of the two. In any case, this is a time when new ideas are explored. Just this in itself will open the door to consideration of a skills inventory system. If, in addition, part of the review or investigation indicated that an inventory should be installed, it becomes a very real requirement. Not only is it a part of reviewing the overall system, but a specific addition.

UNEMPLOYMENT DATA BANKS

A limited skills inventory use has been found at some state and local government levels. Here, those people applying for unemployment benefits are entered into a central file. Employers have access and jobs are matched to people seeking work. In this way certain placements are achieved and unemployment payments reduced, and those involved are once more employed.

Technologically the ability exists to cross-match all openings to all job seekers. It would be a major undertaking, but it is well within the realm of possibility. It could easily be expanded to include not just those out of work, but those interested in changing jobs or positions.

There are often job openings in one city, county or state, and people seeking these same positions in another. Getting the two together has some interesting possibilities. If they are unemployed, this would aid in reducing this problem. Overall, this has an impact on taxes and other immediate monetary considerations.

It also takes into account the better use of one of our major resources—the human resource. If iron ore were needed in one area, and it was available in another, a means of distribution would be arrived at. It makes good economic sense to at least provide a system to notify those involved, of the location and availability of a required resource.

People are a valuable resource and possibly too valuable to go to a total concept of a central data bank or national skills inventory. As with any system of this magnitude, it contains the basic ingredients for abuse. Most of us are torn by the desire to provide a valuable service on the one hand, and fear of creating a monster on the other.

A person who wants to work and is unemployed is someone who needs aid and assistance. By the same token, we want everyone to have the opportunity to use his/her skills and abilities to the fullest.

This then makes both under-employment, and not just unemployment a target for corrective action.

Data banks of all types become subjects of debates and misuse. Those in the private sector as well as those in the public sector have come under scrutiny. There have been problems with improper disclosure and use of some of the information. Laws have been enacted to aid in the control and future operation of these systems.

The problem here is that too much control results in a waste of the human resource, and the ability to provide a positive use of our current technology. How far do we want to go with control or lack of it? What risk do we want to take to utilize our human resources and potentials? There are no totally acceptable answers at the present time. Like most problems in this area, the concerns are complex and multi-faceted.

The trend seems to be to go to the use of central placement concepts. In the future, more of this at all levels of government will become apparent. The movement in this area is slow and cautious. Laws and policies will be required at each step to be certain that the potential for abuse is guarded against. These can act as counter-balancing forces that ultimately result in accurate and controlled operations.

PRIVATE PLACEMENT

Private employment agencies have been making use of the data bank concept quite satisfactorily. These include those agencies and services for both clerical and management or professional placement. There is the possibility that they may be able to meet demands sufficiently so that a government central data bank is not required.

Some of these specialize by industries, others by area, while others are general in nature. Another positive aspect is that they are not necessarily restricted by geographical boundaries. Often, a person will submit a résumé and complete an inventory in one part of the country, and receive an inquiry through the search firm for another area.

Many of the systems now ask to identify the employee's areas of preference, or areas to which he/she would definitely not be interested in going. There are multiple coding systems being employed as the automation of these systems progresses. In the future, these types of search activities will probably become more prevalent. There is a sound network now established that seems to be growing, which is usually a good indicator of where we will be in the future.

The skills inventory concept can be useful to a large and expanding search or placement firm. The concept has several benefits. First, it allows a certain amount of structure to the collection of information on who is in the job market and looking for what type of position.

This structure can be important if there are multiple offices that are geographically dispersed. It is also important if the interviewers are changing or new, as additional offices are opening. It provides consistency in communication, and allows for a more rapid training experience for those entering the firm. As it does with any other organization, the inventory establishes a common language.

It also provides a much wider range of potential applicants for any specific job opening. In past years, someone in the search field often worked on placing whichever résumé was on the top of the stack. Now, if the file is automated, a scan of all possible applicants can be made rather than reliance being made on memory, or on the suggestion of a colleague.

An effort can at least be made to keep the files current. A separation can be made of those people who have been placed, or are no longer actively seeking positions. This can be accomplished by periodic contacts (by phone or return postcard) to enquire if the individual is still actively seeking placement or not. This update system is similar in nature to the periodic updates an employer might conduct on his/her own skills inventory.

Access time can be very important. This has led some of the larger search firms to explore advances in technology and computer applications. The opportunity is there to connect remote sites to each other via terminal. It allows the ability to enquire and update the data bank rapidly, and with a high degree of accuracy. This area of business is highly competitive and these advances may provide the "competitive edge" for those search firms making use of them.

There are advantages to the job seeker, just as there are to an employee in an organization. Most search firms make every effort to protect the confidentiality of those on their files. First, their reputation and source of applicants demand this, and they are guarded about their files because they represent their source of business.

Those in the system receive the additional visibility of being considered by the search firms as they receive information on openings. These firms usually have information sources that job seekers would not begin to possess. In some cases job openings go directly to the firm, or are identified by it, when working with a client before any other recruiting sources are involved.

Certain people believe it is wise to be on file with several of these groups at all times, the idea being that you are available for any attractive opportunity which you might normally be unaware of. This does involve continuous active participation, such as seeking the classified section of the newspaper. Of course, this would be for the person who is employed and just interested in keeping his/her options open. The unemployed job seeker would probably be interested in taking a much more active role.

There seems to be an interest and a market for these types of search firms. Employers find their work valuable, and during peak periods they provide a very vital service. Also, they are useful in locating people with unique skills and talents. The future of these organizations seems secure, and is indeed expanding. The use of new and advanced technology and computers will enhance their performance.

TECHNOLOGICAL ADVANCES

The implications here are interesting and exciting. There are items in progress now which will make the concept of skills inventories even more attractive in the future. One which was discussed earlier was voice inquiries. Here we have the ability to make inquiries using the spoken word. The response can be set up to come back the same way or possibly on a printed listing if so required.

There are also the advances being made in scanning devices for selecting information from printed or written documents. This can be an aid in speeding up the input forms and documents now being used. The individual or employee would not have to follow the rigid format of most existing input forms. Under this concept the person could describe his/her background and let the computers identify the salient points and words. This could provide the benefits of an in-depth interview without the expense of the interviewer.

Technological advances will continue to produce new and useful products. As these become justified, they will become part of the skills inventory package. Skills inventories attracted interest even before the punched card sort systems. New advances that make them easier to use will only expand and enhance their use.

15
SUMMARY AND CONCLUSION

DEVELOPMENT OF MATERIAL

In the past chapters a great deal of material has been covered dealing with the various aspects of skills inventories. This was written in layman's terms and aimed at a broad audience. It was not designed for the data processing professional, but for the manager or the supervisor who needs to understand what skills inventories are all about.

Technical jargon has been avoided wherever possible. When this was impossible, a layman's explanation was attempted. Diagrams and charts were used to try to make the discussion visual and easier to understand. Effort was taken to develop and insert these in areas that normally create questions. The intent was to employ the old adage of a "picture is worth a thousand words."

A great deal of time and effort was spent on the sequence of the chapters. The intent here was to lead the reader through the development into the application stages of skills inventories. However, each chapter on a particular topic was designed to stand alone. In some cases an individual is interested in only selected portions of a topic, and does not wish to be referred to numerous different reference points to find the information regarding the topic. A specific chapter will meet this specific need.

SEQUENCE OF CHAPTERS

The initial sequence of chapters starts with a definition. This is a definition of skills inventories and their uses. Along with this was provided some historical matter relating to their development and use in the past in a business environment. This provided a springboard into considerations of future design and development. Discussion in this area provided some insight into the impact on both the public and private sector.

Provision was then made to review the definition and alternate examples of the individual parts of the skills inventory. This included what we refer to as primary inventory items such as key words, work experience, education, language proficiency, special courses, special projects, vocational licenses, etc. Then we went into the secondary items that can be included—such things as hobbies, social clubs, publications, etc.

The primary and secondary terms were developed as possible diversion points. They were in no way intended to be absolute. A primary item in one inventory might be a secondary item in another inventory, and vice versa. Thinking of the skills inventory in this manner makes it a little easier to group the first time around. As was stressed throughout the book, each organization or business grouping may wish something tailored for their needs.

Since the primary and secondary concept is not truly firm, it opens the way for future creativity. As far as wide use and acceptance are concerned, skills inventories are relatively new. These systems have been around for a number of years, but not in the numbers we see them in today. Readers will, it is hoped, be able to add to this list themselves. As time goes on, priorities in the organizational world change. With this in mind, the concept of primary and secondary becomes what it should be—a starting point. Here is a place to get ideas and understand concepts. Individuals or organizations must determine their own needs and requirements and develop a system accordingly.

There is an art to systems design. Skills inventories certainly are no exception. As you look at the primary or secondary items for your organization, allow the creative juices to flow a bit. Make the selection according to your judgment, and involve the various managers and department heads. This allows participation by those who will be required to give their support. It is through this group process that the skills inventories of the future will be designed and developed.

An entire chapter was devoted to one of the items noted as being of primary importance. This dealt with key words and their use. This category is the one most often reviewed during searches. It is the focal point for preparing candidate lists when attempting to fill an open position.

Samples of both key word structures and the related systems were provided. More than one alternative in setting up key word systems were given. This was aimed at providing the reader with a series of choices for his/her own systems design. It is hoped that this also stimulates thinking, and that those reviewing these sections will be able to develop their own structures to meet their specific needs.

A separate chapter was devoted to input forms. Emphasis was placed on capturing the data, and the most accurate ways of doing this. The in-depth interviewing process was discussed, and the advantages and disadvantages pointed out. The employee completed form, some derivation of which is most commonly found in actual use, was reviewed in considerable detail. The aim here was to put forward the ideal data capture methods available for skills inventories, but then to contrast them to those most commonly used.

The second type in any common system, being processing, was given attention in its proper sequence. Here we explored both manual and machine processing concepts. The always difficult question of when to use automation or computer processing was confronted. This may be somewhat of a rarity, since the easiest thing is to steer away from this topic. Clear rules and policies are not readily available, and trying to establish guidelines can be difficult. Some feel that even broaching the subject can lead to criticism that is hard to defend oneself against.

Most works of any value do not avoid the difficult questions or topics. It is only in trying to deal with them, or at least in recognizing their existence that any gains are made. Throughout the book this point was focused on. The area of skills inventories has been one where many of the issues of a more difficult nature have been avoided. Not only in this chapter, but throughout the book, every effort was made to be candid and frank. The criticism that may be forthcoming will lead to more thought and review on the part of those who are concerned and involved. In the long run, this can lead to better and more sophisticated skills inventory systems.

As was the target throughout, samples were provided. Included are samples of manual systems items as well as automated ones. It is realized that automation is the wave of the future. However, there are still organizations around that can effectively utilize a manual system. Giving some attention to these means that every organization has an opportunity to use a skills inventory if it so chooses.

The third step in any system of output was dealt with. As in the input area, the turnaround document was discussed and samples provided. Regardless of input or output, the turnaround document makes a significant contribution to any system. It is of particular value in a skills inventory system, because the employee often completes the form. This precludes the requirement of having multiple forms, and the related problems of distribution and mixup.

Internal design considerations were reviewed. These included such things as determining what terms the organization is most familiar with, and also explored methods of determining a particular organization's set of terms and key words. Emphasis was placed on the involvement of management and others within the organization. They are going to have to live with the system in the future. This being so, it is important to get them involved early. By doing this, we increase the possibility of future understanding and support of the system.

The importance of tying the skills inventory to the requisition system was pointed out. It is mentioned a number of times throughout this book, and it forces a look at the organization policy of hiring from within. If all requisitions are tested against the skills inventory before going to outside hiring, this tells us several things: It says there is a strong policy of promotion from within, and it also indicates that the skills inventory has been given a position of importance within the organization.

External purchase considerations were treated as a separate entity. The "make or buy" considerations are definitely here and on the increase. There are excellent packaged skills inventory systems available. The competition in this marketplace is on the increase. Several years ago, there was no choice. If you wanted a skills inventory, you designed your own or selected from the few systems then being marketed. This is no longer the case.

Information on where to go to find a skills inventory for sale was discussed. In addition, procedures to check out and analyze this purchase decision was reviewed. Systems selection can be very important, since it is often a relatively long commitment. It should not be entered into lightly, nor without the help and assistance of an organization's technical group.

Modification of an outside package is another consideration that is often overlooked. Details regarding possible discussions with vendor/consultants were reviewed. There are modification considerations prior to purchase, and those after purchase that have to be taken into account.

Too often, a system is selected without any provision being made for the future. We know there will be changes and enhancements as technology and the entire state of the art moves forward. Only by taking these into account and preparing for them in the beginning, can we insure they will be provided for. If this is not done the system is programmed for failure and abandonment. As with any other aspect of the organization, the skills inventory must continue to grow and evolve if it is to survive.

There is a third option that was treated in a separate chapter. This dealt with the combination of internal design and external purchase. A system does not have to be totally designed internally, or brought from an outside source. With this realization, our horizons expand tremendously. It allows someone considering purchasing a skills inventory a much wider range of alternatives.

Each organization possesses its strengths and weaknesses. They may exist in the technical areas or in the administrative side. The combination concept allows us to focus on these. Another way of saying this might be to use internal strengths, and purchase our weaknesses. Of course, the first step is to critically analyze what they are.

It can be a painful process for an organization to admit it has weaknesses, just as it is for an individual to do so. In both cases, this can be a valuable occurrence if undertaken properly. It is possible that we may want to employ an outside consultant or third party to aid in this. It is an objective review which is being sought. Achieving this allows the organization to honestly evaluate its options. Being able to do this allows selection of the proper mix of internal design and external purchase.

Also, there was a review of the actual purchase or an external consulting agreement. The concept of what is a vendor and what is a consultant sometimes becomes blurred. In fact, sometimes the consultants and vendors are confused about their own roles. An effort was made to provide some definition in this area. Proper use and interface with these resources can be very important. Skills inventories, as with any other system, have become complex. The outside resources of vendors and consultants, if used properly, can aid in overcoming an organization's lack of knowledge or expertise. They can provide the link with the latest advances in technology. Through their experience, they can aid management in avoiding costly mistakes that others have made.

A good deal of consideration was given to the impact of technology. It is this area which has aided greatly in the expansion in use of skills inventories. In the future, it will be technology which aids in moving the concept even further forward. Technology is moving ever more rapidly, as one advance provides the fuel or opens a door for others. Predictions of the future see technology moving ahead at geometric rates.

In the chapter dealing with the impact of technology, several significant factors were covered. First, a part of the historical development in the computer area was reviewed. Though all inventories are not computerized, a large number of the systems of significant size are computer based. Early computer systems, as with present systems, have had their problems. Today's systems are definitely more responsive to the needs of skills inventories, and tomorrow's will be even more so.

Computer terminals were focused upon as one of the major technological advances in the area. They have provided those dealing with and using skills inventories with additional power and capability. The fact that they are more flexible in use as well as physically portable has expanded their value in the area of skills inventory support. As new computer based systems are developed, it appears that provision for terminal capability will accompany this change.

Mini computer systems are on the scene and have some advantages for skills inventory users. One possibility lies in greater user control over input, processing and output. This of course will hinge on organization policy and structure. Still, the possibility of greater user control becomes more of a reality. With this control comes the ability to better schedule the products involved. This in turn, if properly applied, may lead to better and faster response time to management's requests for inventory products.

Microfilm has been around a long time. It has also had significant use in supporting skills inventory systems. Rather than having become an obsolete tool, it too has continued to keep pace through advances in technology. In fact, with postage rates rising, it provides a convenient method of transporting information at reduced costs. New microfilm-based systems and concepts are being developed. Recently, new devices have appeared which allow more sorting capability and search capability to be tied into a microfilm system.

Skills inventories are no different from any other management system, there is a cost to using them. A chapter has been devoted to reviewing the implication of this. First there are important factors that must be identified and defined, so that the magnitude or cost impact can be analyzed.

There are certain basic considerations for determining the optimum skills inventory cost for an individual firm or organization. In fact, there are many ways to approach this consideration of cost and get very reliable figures. It appears it is a little more difficult to identify the benefit aspect of skills inventories. Benefits seems to fall into more of an intangible category. All of these factors enter into the picture and are part of the management's concern when making a decision on using a skills inventory.

One chapter has been devoted to the maximum use of a system. Management needs to know when and how to use a skills inventory system. A system can be the best in the world, but if not implemented and used properly it will be of little use.

The types of communications to introduce the system were discussed in detail. Most organizations of any size have a "house organ" or company newsletter. The effective handling of this can be important to both introducing and supporting the system. It can be used as a device to encourage employee participation, and to explain the successes the system has experienced.

The problems with both voluntary and mandatory participation were reviewed. The concern over privacy legislation has an impact on the skills inventory. There are approaches to confronting and overcoming these concerns. Voluntary participation is, of course, one of the ways of achieving this. However, voluntary participation brings with it a unique set of problems of its own. These are explored and discussed.

Overall, management has many choices in presenting the system to employees and gaining their acceptance. As was discussed, the ideal way to approach this problem is to gain employee support and acceptance. When they are interested, and truly supportive of the system, this enhances the likelihood of success.

In addition to the house organ, management has available many tools to gain interest and support. Some of the ones noted were the use of the introductory films and related audio visual material. Proper preparation and presentation of staff meeting material by supervisors was noted as another effective method. The main theme that was stressed was support from the top management. A skills inventory system has a much better chance of achieving success if it has top down support. This shows the employees that management is serious about the new system and is not just giving it lip service.

There are many positive aspects of skills inventories which can and should be stressed. These include not being lost in the system, opportunity to be considered for promotion, greater overall visibility, etc. However, it was stressed that false expectations should not be built up. Employees should be told that participation in the system does not guarantee promotion, transfer, new job assignments, or anything else. They must also be told that while it may aid in assuring that individuals are considered on a fair and equitable basis, there cannot of course be any guarantees that every person who is considered, will be selected.

Another chapter was written to provide some insight into a very pertinent area dealing with the reasons why some skills inventories have failed. This was felt necessary, since an understanding of why systems have not succeeded may aid us in finding ways to make our system work.

It was pointed out that failure of a skills inventory, or any other system, can come in two forms. The first being the most obvious, but that lack of use also constitutes a failure situation. In either case, the reasons behind these occurrences are worth studying and reviewing. There is something to be learned from failure that can aid in future success.

The last chapter was aimed at reviewing two questions which continue to arise anytime skills inventories are discussed. First, is their relationship to manpower planning, and second is the future of these types of systems.

Many times skills inventory systems are viewed as *the* manpower planning system. In reality skills inventory systems are, or can be, *one* of the tools of manpower planning. The actual topic of manpower planning is much broader than just a skills inventory system. This is a common misconception which has been dealt with in this section.

The future of skills inventory systems seems very positive. It is felt that more systems are appearing and will continue to appear in the coming years. There are many factors in this area which are explored in depth. One that is noted is the ease smaller firms have in obtaining access to computers. This makes the application of computerized skills inventories much more feasible.

Another point that is brought out is the availability of package systems. More of these are coming onto the market each year. Many of the general personnel packages include a skills inventory as one of the standard items. Those firms picking up such a system automatically gain an inventory. In addition, some of the older systems are bringing out inventories as additions to, or enhancements of, their existing systems.

INDEX

INDEX

affirmative action, 192, 201-202
alternate consultant uses, 123

basic output, 67
batch processing, 135
biography, 1-2, 46, 67-69
build-up phase, 189-190
business use, 8-13

calculators, 11 13
candidate list, 69-70
central data bank, 17
classical manpower planning, 192-194
compatability of terms, 94
competitive advantages, 98, 100
completion time, 112-114
computer output microfilm (COM), 143-144
computer rooms, 14-15
consultant/vendors, 103-112, 117-129, 199, 211-212
costs, 11, 13, 16, 129, 145-167, 187-188, 200-201
CRT, 138

data base, 65
data capture, 65
data-entry professional, 184
data system, 133

Delphi method, 28
designing the form, 52-53
detailed contracts, 115-116
developing internally, 101-102
distribution patterns, 80-81

economic upswings, 188-190
education, 19-20, 23-24, 68, 208
emphasizing positive, 179-180
employee completion, 49-50, 52
employee data sheet, 1-2
employment agencies, 203-205
estimates, 163-165
external listings, 11

failures, 181-190
false expectations, 179
fine tuning, 181
firm model, 194
form distribution, 80-82

house organ, 177-178
human resource planning, 191

ideal information, 45, 48, 50-52
ideal match, 10
index cards, 59
index lists, 69-73
information gathering, 44-48

219

Index

input forms, 43-55
intangible benefits, 188
integration of computers, 133-136
interviewing, 48
introducing system, 174-180

job classifications, 145-146
job posting, 198
joint venture, 124-125

key words, 19-21, 23, 30-42, 68, 73, 187, 208
   definition, 30-32
   organization requirements, 40-41
   requisition system, 41-42
   space allocation, 38-40
   structuring, 32-38

language, 1, 3, 19-20, 22-23, 29, 40, 68, 71, 208
locating vendors/consultants, 107-108

make or buy, 101-116, 165-166, 210
management goals, 166-167
management systems, 114, 133-134
manpower planning, 191-206, 215
manpower planning tools, 196-199
manual or machine, 130-132
manual methods, 58-61
measurable goals, 111-112
microfilm, 64, 143-144, 213
milestone chart, 112-114
miniaturization, 14
mini computers, 140, 142, 213
misuse, 16-17
mix of skills, 57

N.I.H. factor, 118

optimum inventory, 172, 174
organizational terms, 83-84
organization involvement, 125-126
organization's language, 85-86

output forms, 65-82
outside candidates, 94-100
outside candidate system, 96-97
over-engineering, 184, 186

package systems, 102-103, 215
participation, 16
pilot questionnaire, 184-186
pilot test, 79-80, 159-162
primary inventory, 19, 27-29
privacy, 175
private placement, 203-205
professional certificate, 1, 3
promotion from within, 91-92
psychological reinforcement, 78-79
punched cards, 10-11, 133, 135, 206
purchasing a package system, 102-103

requisition system, 41-42, 88-90, 168-169
resident search expert, 169-173
rule of thumb, 57-58

salary information, 137
sample firms, 66-67
search request, 169-170
secondary search criteria, 27-29
security, 119-120
selecting parts, 27
seller's market, 189
sequence of chapters, 207-215
skills mix, 192-193
software packages, 122-123
software service, 128-129
special courses, 19-20, 23-25, 68, 208
special projects 19-20, 23, 25-26, 208
staff planning, 191
storage and processing, 56-64
supervisory reluctance, 92-94
systems triangle, 134
systems visibility, 154-157

technological advances, 205-206

terminal access, 63
terminal files, 11
terminals, 136-142, 212
training, 4-5, 125, 197
turnaround document, 53-55, 75-79, 210
typewriter terminals, 63, 138-139

unemployment data banks, 202-203
updates, 72, 75, 77-78, 127-128

upward mobility, 189

vocational licenses, 19-20, 23, 26-27, 68, 208
voluntary participation, 214,

war baby boom, 194
work experience, 1, 3, 19-20, 45-47, 68, 208